The
P·L·A·I·N
& Fancy
MUSTARD
COOKBOOK

·RITA CALVERT·

The
East Woods
Press

The East Woods Press   Charlotte, N.C.

Library of Congress Cataloging-in-Publication Data

Calvert, Rita, 1953–
    The plain and fancy mustard cookbook.

    Includes index.
    1. Cookery (Mustard) I. Title
TX819.M87C35   1986   641.6'384   86-45578
ISBN 0-88742-100-8

Copyedited by Linda Benefield
Cover Design by Cindi Kerr
Illustrations by Carol Raab
Typography by Raven Type
Printed in the United States of America

East Woods Press Books
Fast & McMillan Publishers, Inc.
429 East Boulevard
Charlotte, NC 28203

In memory of Nana,
who taught me the appreciation
of "real" food, simple or complex

Acknowledgments

Many thanks to my editor, Sue Headrick, to Pat Coughlin for being a sleuth on research, and to Carol Raab for illustrations. They handled the deadlines like champs.

And much appreciation to those fellow mustard enthusiasts who supplied inspiration.

Contents

Introduction

I love mustard! Oh, not just the bright yellow stuff which is nonchalantly squirted on hotdogs and hamburgers (although a hotdog at the ballpark or the circus just wouldn't be the same without it).

Think of all the types available to us today—silky or coarse; mild to hot; seasoned with wine, spices, fruits, beer and herbs; ranging in color from the ubiquitous yellow to pale creams to the darkest of browns. Dozens and dozens of varieties have come on the market in the past five years or so. Many are sold nationally through specialty food shops or gourmet grocery stores, some are marketed regionally, and others are prepared in restaurants and at home by adventurous cooks. People now collect mustards, much as they choose wines for the cellar, each one picked for its particular properties.

As the oldest condiment known to man (excepting only salt and pepper), mustard is today taking its place as a basic element in creative cooking, instead of just being dolloped over prepared meats, sausages or cheeses. It's fun to cook with mustard. It adds zing to every dining course, from soups and salad dressings to meat, fish and poultry. It helps make sauces, glazes or marinades deeper and more dimensional, changing them into complex entities in a matter of seconds.

My interest in mustard began with my Pennsylvania childhood and my grandmother's kitchen. Though not Amish, Nana, a short, comfy lady whose kitchen was the focal point of all social activity, was certainly influenced by the Pennsylvania Dutch style of cooking. I vividly remember making the rounds of farmer's markets and festivals in York and Lancaster, admiring the shining piles of tomatoes, apples, corn and other fruits and vegetables. I was always encouraged to help Nana with meal preparation . . . nothing fancy, mind you, but solid farm-style cooking which combined fresh fruits and vegetables, plain meats and poultry and, of course, some form of the traditional seven sweets and seven sours—relishes, mustards, condiments, butters and sauces so dear to the hearts of the Amish and traditionally found at all meals. It was years, in fact, before I realized that having one's eggs with tomato relish every morning was somewhat unusual.

Unlike many in my field, I didn't decide early on to become a chef. After high school, I was more interested in design and modeling. Eventually, like so many of my generation, I migrated to California. I was just in time for the West Coast food explosion of the 1970s. Exhilarated by the abundance of foodstuffs, the creativity of the young chefs and the various nouveau cuisines, I found a new ambition had crystallized and I jumped in. Pantry person, student in specialty cooking classes, baker, luncheon chef, co-manager of a country club and finally, owner of my own restaurant, Cedar Street Cafe in Santa Cruz, situated in a restored Victorian house and art gallery. Here I was surrounded by fresh herbs, flowers, veggies and a staff of wonderfully creative young people.

I began making my own spicy, hot and sweet mustard and placed crocks of it with fresh bread sticks on the tables. Our customers loved it. People would sit there and eat it all . . . some even put it on their salads as dressing. And that's how Calvert's Cedar Street specialty products were born. The decision to market these products nationally came after I moved back to the East Coast with my new husband. I experimented with the marvelous Southern crops in North Carolina, such as blueberries and pecans, and recreated some traditional regional favorites. Today, the company produces six mustards (including the Original and the highly popular Bumpy Beer type), three vinaigrettes, two relishes and a Champagne Sauce for poultry and fish. Not quite "seven sweets and seven sours" yet, but we're working on it!

Just what is mustard?

Basically, it is a condiment derived from the seeds of *Brassica juncea* (brown/black) or *Brassica hirta* (white), which are either pressed into oil or powdered. Mustard is low in calories (with less than ten calories in a spoonful of the Dijon type) and high in protein and minerals, including calcium, magnesium, phosphorus, potassium and niacin.

Although mustard may take on almost any flavor, spice or herb, it mainly appears in four different forms: the whole seeds, both brown and white; oil, used mainly in Middle Eastern and West Asian cooking; dry powder; and prepared. Early Egyptians chewed a few seeds with their meals to give flavor. In the nineteenth century, the English developed a method to separate the seeds from the hulls, and then reduced the seeds to a powder, which is still a basic part of the market today. Pressing the seeds into a pungent oil produces a polyunsaturated product which is a mainstay of the Indian and Pakistani diet, along with ghee, clarified butter.

The prepared mustards available to us today generally fall into the following categories:

American	A rather bland, bright yellow product incorporating lots of turmeric and vinegar
Dijon	A smooth, clean, sharp mustard from France, not particularly hot, and marvelous in sauces
English	A fiery version, usually mixed with water, ranging from smooth to grainy, sometimes including the hulls, available both in powder and prepared versions
Chinese	Hot, hot, hot, whether in powder or paste form. Great for clearing out the sinuses
German	Generally a medium to dark brown, mild and sometimes slightly sweet, usually crunchy
Scandinavian	Sweet/sour in flavor, usually containing seeds or husks and wonderful with smoked fish
Creole	Hot and eyeopening, a combination of French and Spanish styles
Spanish	Mild to hot, sometimes containing sherry and/or peppercorns

Flavored mustards are generally a Dijon style combined with any herb, spice, wine, beer, fruit or vegetable you can imagine.

You may, of course, make your very own mustard, starting with mustard powder and water and adding your choice of flavors, or by processing a combination of mustard seed, vinegar, dry mustard, water, wine and spices.

The *Plain and Fancy Mustard Cookbook* was written to challenge your creativity . . . to ask you to experiment, taste, try new combinations and recognize the unusual merit mustard adds to the marriage of food flavors.

Try the recipes; experiment with the many mustard types. Should you have a less than perfect outcome, don't despair. I once scorched a 300-gallon commercial batch of mustard which had to be tearfully dispatched to the dumpster. Fortunately, the experience didn't dull my enthusiasm. Learn, be challenged and above all, have fun and eat well. Use mustard to add that special spice to your life!

HORS D'OEUVRES DIPS & SPREADS

Key Ingredient: Cheese   Courses: Main, side
Servings: Eight   Food Group: Dairy
Cuisine: French   Temperature: Hot
Meals: Brunch, dinner, party   Time: 30 minutes

Monique's Fondue

¼   cup cognac

1   cup dry white wine

3   tablespoons spicy hot and sweet mustard

1   teaspoon chives

1   tablespoon lemon juice (fresh)

1   teaspoon oregano, crushed

2   cloves garlic, minced

8   ounces Emmenthaler cheese, shredded

4   ounces Gruyère cheese, shredded

     freshly ground black pepper

     fresh French bread, cubed

Place first seven ingredients in fondue pot over medium heat. Gradually add cheeses while stirring. Add pepper, and keep warm on low heat. Spear bread cubes with fondue fork and dip in cheese mixture.

Key Ingredient: Whipping cream	Course: Hors d'oeuvre
Servings: Eight	Food Group: Dairy
Cuisine: American	Temperatures: Cold, room
Meals: Dinner, party	Time: 30 minutes

Kasseri Cheese Mousse

A delicate and elegant hors d'oeuvre. Time does not include overnight refrigeration.

2	cups heavy whipping cream
1	teaspoon unflavored gelatin
2	tablespoons Calvados or apple brandy
2	tablespoons spicy hot and sweet mustard
12	ounces Kasseri cheese, finely grated
1	teaspoon rosemary, chopped very fine, and additional fresh sprigs

Whip cream in a chilled bowl until stiff. Refrigerate. Soften gelatin in Calvados. Heat over low heat until gelatin is dissolved. Let cool slightly.

Gently fold gelatin mixture, mustard, cheese and rosemary evenly into whipped cream. Line a 4-cup mold with plastic film wrap. Place fresh sprigs of rosemary on bottom of mold. Place whipped cream cheese mixture in mold. Cover and refrigerate overnight, if possible.

Unmold, remove film, and surround with fresh seasonal fruit, bread sticks and wafer-thin Swedish crackers.

Key Ingredient: Corned beef
Servings: Yields 2¾ cups
Cuisine: American
Meals: Dip, topping

Course: Hors d'oeuvre
Food Group: Meat, Dairy
Temperature: Cold
Time: 10 minutes (does not include chilling time)

"Easy Bert's" Dip

Many of my customers and fellow mustard enthusiasts have shared their inspirations with me. This is one of those delightful recipes.

1	12-ounce can corned beef
½	cup dill pickle cubes
1	medium onion, minced
2	tablespoons spicy hot and sweet mustard
4	tablespoons mayonnaise
1	teaspoon horseradish
½	cup sour cream

In a food processor, blend ingredients very well. Chill for at least 2 hours before serving. Delicious with fresh crunchy vegetables, rye breadsticks or for topping a baked potato.

"From three things may the Lord preserve us:
From valets much too proud to serve us;
From women smeared with heavy fard, good grief!
From lack of mustard when we eat corned beef."
　　　　　—From Food, *by Waverly Root,*
　　　　　　　translated from the French

Key Ingredient: Cheese	Course: Main
Servings: Eight	Food Group: Grain
Cuisine: Cretian	Temperature: Hot
Meals: Brunch, lunch	Time: 1 hour and 30 minutes

Cretian Roulade

This makes a lovely brunch dish or luncheon entrée. The flavors, influenced by the island of Crete, lend an exotic note.

	French bread dough (enough to make one loaf), freshly made or frozen
3	tablespoons spicy hot and sweet mustard mixed with 1 teaspoon poppy seeds
16	ounces large curd cottage cheese (or ricotta)
10	ounces frozen chopped spinach, thawed and squeezed dry
1	cup diced ham
4	scallions, chopped
½	teaspoon oregano
2	cloves garlic, minced
1	cup mozzarella cheese, shredded or grated

Let French dough rise once. Punch down, and after letting it rest 10 minutes, roll into an 8-by-12-inch rectangle. Spread with mustard and poppy seed mixture. Mix next six ingredients together. Sprinkle grated cheese over bread dough. Place filling mixture down long side of dough and roll up. Place seam side down on a greased baking sheet and tuck ends under. Brush or spray with water, and make three diagonal slashes on top of roulade. Bake in a 375° preheated oven for 25 minutes. Turn over and bake 10 more minutes to brown bottom. Let rest 10 minutes before cutting. Freezes beautifully.

Key Ingredient: Shrimp   Courses: Hors d'oeuvre, appetizer
Servings: Four   Food Group: Seafood
Cuisine: American   Temperature: Hot
Meals: Dinner, party   Time: 15 minutes

Shrimp Butter

Shrimp butter gives even a plain dish subtle elegance. Try filling fresh mushroom caps or tomato halves and broiling. Use it to top grilled or broiled chicken or fish. It is elegant served simply on thin slices of dense bread.

¼	pound shrimp, cooked until pink, and shelled
2	cloves garlic
1	tablespoon fresh parsley
1	tablespoon spicy hot and sweet mustard
½	teaspoon chives
	freshly ground black pepper and salt to taste
	grated rind of one lemon
½	pound sweet butter (two sticks), soft and cut into chunks

Place all ingredients but butter in a food processor or blender and process until finely chopped. Add butter and process until mixed well. This can be done by hand, but fine chopping is necessary to make a paste of the ingredients.

Key Ingredient: Cheese   Course: Main
Servings: Six   Food Group: Grain, Dairy, Meat
Cuisine: Italian   Temperature: Hot
Meals: Lunch, dinner   Time: 45 minutes

Nuovo Calzone (Enclosed Pizza)

French bread dough (enough for two loaves). Fresh or frozen dough may be used.

4   ounces Kasseri cheese, finely chopped

4   ounces mozzarella, finely chopped

4   ounces feta cheese, crumbled

½   cup Canadian bacon, chopped (Kielbasa sausage may be substituted)

4   tablespoons scallions, finely chopped

1   tablespoon parsley, finely chopped

1   egg, beaten

4   tablespoons spicy hot and sweet mustard mixed with 1 teaspoon fresh basil

   freshly ground pepper to taste

1   egg, beaten

Allow French bread dough to rise once. While it is rising, combine cheeses, Canadian bacon, green onion, parsley, egg and pepper, and set aside.

Punch down dough, divide into sixths, and roll each section into a 7-inch circle, one at a time. Spread each with 2 teaspoons of the mustard and basil mixture and place 1/6 of the filling in center of each circle. Moisten edges with beaten egg and fold over to form a half moon. Crimp edges to seal. Place on baking sheet and refrigerate to prevent rising. Repeat this process with each section. Spray the outside of the pastry with water to form a crunchy crust and make two 1-inch slashes in each to permit air to escape. Bake in a 425° preheated oven for 20 minutes or until golden brown.

Key Ingredient: Mixed
Servings: Four (or eight as an hors d'oeuvre)
Cuisine: Armenian
Meals: Lunch, hors d'oeuvre

Courses: Main, first
Food Group: Meat, Grain
Temperature: Cold
Time: 20 minutes, plus 1 hour chilling time

Lavosh Sandwich Spirals

If Lavosh crackers are not available, large flour tortillas or even large matzo crackers may be substituted using the same process. When using flour tortillas, be extra careful so as not to tear.

K. Fowler's Spread:

1	tablespoon spicy hot and sweet mustard
1	small can pitted black olives, drained (or olive paste, if available in specialty food departments)
2	tablespoons olive oil
1	clove fresh garlic
1	tablespoon sour cream or mascarpone cheese, if available
2	large Lavosh crackers, at least 10 inches in diameter
8	ounces veal or turkey breast, thinly sliced (4 ounces per roll)
8	ounces Provolone cheese, thinly sliced (4 ounces per roll)
1	cup fresh spinach leaves, finely shredded
2	medium tomatoes, thinly sliced

Dip Lavosh crackers quickly in cold water to soften. Keeping them flat, place between clean towels to absorb extra moisture while softening.

Make spread by placing olives (or olive paste), olive oil and garlic in food processor or blender. Purée to a paste-like consistency. Mix purée with mustard and sour cream (or mascarpone).

Spread half of olive mixture on each softened Lavosh. Top with thin layers of veal or turkey breast, spinach, tomato and cheese. Roll up gently but tightly. Wrap each roll securely in plastic wrap. Refrigerate for at least one hour.

When ready to serve, slice into 1-inch pieces.

Key Ingredient: Yogurt   Temperatures: Cold, room
Servings: Six to eight   Time: 5 minutes

The Bumper

8	ounces plain yogurt
3	tablespoons spicy hot and sweet mustard
1	teaspoon mustard seeds
½	teaspoon poppy seeds
2	slices fresh ginger, minced very fine
1	tablespoon honey
¼	cup chopped scallions
2	teaspoons tamari or soy sauce

Mix all ingredients together. May be kept in refrigerator for up to two weeks.
Lovely to top baked or sautéed chicken breasts. Great as a dip for Oriental finger foods such as egg rolls, fried wonton and rumaki.
Serving size may vary according to sauce's use.

Key Ingredient: Cream cheese   Temperatures: Hot, cold, room
Servings: Eight   Time: 10 minutes
Cuisine: Italian

Nuovo Spreadables

This is a special addition to breads, crackers and Lavosh. Try stuffing raw vegetables with this mixture. Top a baked potato with it for an Italian spud!

8	ounces cream cheese, softened
3	tablespoons spicy hot and sweet mustard
½	teaspoon fresh basil leaf, chopped
⅓	cup chopped black olives
¼	cup pimentos
2	tablespoons capers
1	small shallot, minced

Beat mustard into softened cream cheese. Add remaining ingredients.
Serving size may vary according to sauce's use.

SOUPS

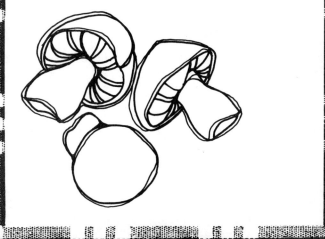

Key Ingredient: Clams
Servings: Four to six
Cuisine: American
Meals: Appetizer, lunch, dinner, brunch

Courses: First, main
Food Group: Seafood, Vegetable
Temperature: Hot
Time: 30–45 minutes

Clam, Mushroom and Spinach Soup

This soup is a delightful break from the proverbial New England Clam Chowder. The clams and creamy comfort are still there, but the mushrooms and spinach add an exotic touch.

4   tablespoons butter

8   ounces fresh mushrooms, sliced

6   scallions, cleaned and sliced

3   tablespoons flour

2   cups clam juice (use reserved juice from drained clams)

3   cups half-and-half
    freshly ground black pepper

3   tablespoons spicy hot and sweet mustard

2   cloves fresh garlic, pressed

6   ounces fresh spinach leaves, cleaned and coarsely chopped

3   tablespoons dry vermouth

2   6½-ounce cans chopped clams, drained

¼   teaspoon salt or to taste
    Red Bell Pepper Purée (recipe follows)

Melt butter in large saucepan over medium-high heat. When hot, add mushrooms and scallions and sauté for 3 minutes. Stir in flour and coat vegetables. Slowly pour in clam juice while stirring constantly. Stir in half-and-half, mustard, garlic and pepper. Add chopped spinach.

Continue cooking over medium heat but do not let soup reach a boil. After cooking for 10 minutes, lower heat and simmer 20 minutes. Meanwhile, make Red Bell Pepper Purée:

3   red peppers, roasted and peeled

1   teaspoon Dijon-style mustard
    dash tabasco

1   egg yolk

½   cup vegetable oil

Roast peppers by turning them over a gas flame until blackened or by turning under a broiler until charred. Place in a brown paper bag and close tightly. Allow to "sweat" in bag for 15 minutes. When cool, peel and remove seeds.

Place peppers, egg yolk, mustard and tabasco in blender or food processor. Purée while slowly pouring in oil.

After making purée, add clams, vermouth and salt to creamy spinach and vegetable mixture. Cook until clams are warm. Ladle into bowls and top each with a tablespoon of Red Pepper Purée. Draw through the puree with a knife to make a decorative swirl design.

Key Ingredient: Pecans   Courses: First, soup
Servings: Six   Food Group: Vegetable
Cuisine: American/Southern style   Temperature: Hot
Meals: Lunch, dinner, appetizer   Time: 45 minutes

Bourbon-Laced Pecan Soup

This is a contemporary recipe that just reeks of old Southern romance.

4   leeks, green parts removed, cleaned and split lengthwise

6   tablespoons butter

3   tablespoons flour

1½   cups pecans, coarsely chopped and toasted

3   cups chicken stock, homemade or tinned

2   cups half-and-half

2 to 3 tablespoons bourbon

1   tablespoon Dijon-style mustard

½   teaspoon tarragon

dash nutmeg

salt and white pepper to taste

Slice leeks crosswise very thinly. In large heavy saucepan, melt butter and sauté leeks over medium-high heat for 5 minutes. Add pecans and cook 3 more minutes. Add flour gradually and stir well. Very slowly, while stirring constantly, pour in chicken stock and then half-and-half. Add mustard, tarragon and nutmeg. Cook over medium heat while stirring (do not let boil). Lower heat and simmer for 20 minutes. Add bourbon, stir well, and serve.

Key Ingredients: Carrots and beets
Servings: Four to six
Cuisine: American
Meals: Lunch, dinner

Courses: First, soup
Food Group: Vegetable
Temperature: Cold
Time: 1 hour. Includes cooking but not chilling time. May be made in advance or even frozen.

Mom's Chilled Magenta Soup

This soup is a delicious surprise and is probably the most beautiful color you will ever see.

12 ounces fresh beets, scrubbed, ends removed, chopped

12 ounces fresh carrots, scrubbed and chopped

2½ cups fresh or tinned chicken stock

⅓ cup fresh lemon juice

½ teaspoon nutmeg

¾ teaspoon salt and pepper

4 teaspoons Dijon-style mustard

¾ cup sour cream

Place beets, carrots, chicken stock, lemon juice, salt, pepper and nutmeg in a non-aluminum saucepan. Bring to a full boil and then lower heat, cover, and simmer for 45 minutes. When vegetables are very tender, place with a small amount of stock in a blender or food processor. Purée until completely smooth.

Add the rest of the chicken stock and mustard while still processing. Adjust seasoning. Chill for at least 6 hours or overnight.

Ladle into individual bowls and top with equal portions of sour cream.

Key Ingredient: Onions   Courses: Appetizer, soup
Servings: Six to eight   Food Group: Vegetable
Cuisine: American   Temperature: Hot
Meals: Lunch, dinner   Time: 1 hour and 30 minutes

George's American Onion Soup

This is one of the finest recipes for French onion soup that I have ever tasted and was truly a favorite in my restaurant. It was named after the guy who loved the onions, cheese and the mustard!

4	tablespoons sweet butter
2	tablespoons olive oil
2	pounds sweet yellow onions (Vidalia onions, if possible), peeled and sliced
2	cloves garlic, minced
½	teaspoon salt
½	teaspoon sugar
2	tablespoons flour
2	quarts strong chicken stock
1	large bay leaf
¼	cup dry red wine
2	tablespoons cognac or brandy
6–8	slices French bread, dried in a low oven until very crisp
3	tablespoons Dijon-style mustard
1	cup grated Gruyère cheese
½	cup grated Teleme cheese
¼	cup grated Parmesan cheese

Heat butter and oil. Sauté onions over medium-high heat until they begin to brown, about 15 to 20 minutes. Add garlic, salt and sugar. Sprinkle flour over onions and stir. Add chicken stock and bay leaf and simmer 30 minutes. Add wine and brandy and simmer 10 minutes.

Spread crisp bread slices with an equal portion of mustard. Pour soup into ovenproof bowls and float one bread slice in each. Mix Gruyère and Teleme cheeses and sprinkle over top of soup. Then sprinkle with Parmesan. Place in a 400° oven and bake until cheese is golden and crispy.

Key Ingredient: Tomatoes   Courses: Appetizer, soup
Servings: Eight   Food Group: Vegetable
Cuisine: American   Temperature: Hot
Meals: Lunch, dinner   Time: 45 minutes

Lori B.'s Dilled Tomato Soup

6	tablespoons sweet butter
2	medium purple onions, peeled and sliced
1	quart fresh or canned chicken stock
2	cups fresh tomatoes, peeled, seeded and diced
2	cloves garlic, minced
2	tablespoons fresh lemon juice
2	tablespoons Dijon-style mustard
1	teaspoon dill weed
1	tablespoon horseradish
2	teaspoons Worcestershire sauce
	salt and pepper to taste

Melt butter in a non-aluminum saucepan and sauté onions over medium heat until translucent, about 8 minutes. Add chicken stock, tomatoes, garlic and lemon juice. Heat to boiling. Lower heat and simmer for 30 minutes. Add mustard, dill weed, horseradish and Worcestershire. Transfer in batches to blender or food processor fitted with a steel blade and process until puréed. A small spring of fresh dill makes a lovely garnish.

Key Ingredient: Carrots   Course: Soup
Servings: Four to six   Food Group: Vegetable
Cuisine: American   Temperature: Cold
Meals: Brunch, lunch   Time: 1 hour and 15 minutes

Chilled Carrot Velvet

This cool soup has everything: nutrition, virtually no calories and elegance in its simplicity. What more can you ask?

3	cups orange juice
2	cups chopped fresh carrots
1	leek, cleaned and chopped
2	teaspoons lemon juice
	salt to taste
2	tablespoons Dijon-style mustard mixed with 1 teaspoon chives
2	teaspoons freshly grated ginger
¾	cup plain yogurt
	fresh, thin orange slices

Heat orange juice in a non-aluminum saucepan just to boiling. Add carrots and leek and cook over medium heat until very tender, about 45 minutes. Remove from heat, and stir in mustard and chive mixture and fresh ginger. Purée this mixture in a blender or food processor. Refrigerate. When chilled, blend in yogurt and stir well. Place in individual serving bowls and add a dollop more of mustard and chive mixture on top of each serving soup. Garnish with a small, thin, fresh orange slice.

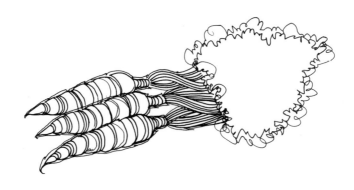

SALADS

Key Ingredient: Sausage
Servings: Four
Cuisine: Italian
Meals: Lunch, dinner

Courses: Salad, side
Food Group: Meat, Vegetable, Grain
Temperature: Cold
Time: 1 hour

Mostaciolli Salad Sardinia

Arugala leaves or one head Boston lettuce,
cleaned and dried

2 sweet Italian sausages

1 jar marinated artichoke hearts, drained

1 small purple onion

½ cup matchstick slices of fresh fennel (or
1½ teaspoons crushed fennel seed)

¼ cup Basic Vinaigrette Recipe (refer to Index)

2 cloves garlic, pressed

½ teaspoon anchovy paste

2 teaspoons Dijon-style mustard

3 tablespoons flat Italian parsley, chopped (if not
available, use regular parsley)

½ pound mostaciolli pasta, cooked al dente,
drained

½ cup Basic Vinaigrette (see Index)

Boil sausage for 10 minutes and slice. Line platter or serving plates with lettuce, and chill. Mix cooked sausage, artichoke hearts, onion, fennel, ¼ cup vinaigrette, garlic, anchovy paste, mustard and parsley together and chill for at least 30 minutes.

Toss pasta with remaining vinaigrette and place on lettuce leaves. Top pasta with sausage mixture. Fresh Italian plum tomato wedges sliced lengthwise make a nice garnish.

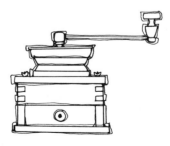

Key Ingredient: Ham   Courses: Salad
Servings: Four   Food Group: Meat, Vegetable
Cuisine: American   Temperature: Cold
Meals: Lunch   Time: 30 minutes

Sunshine Salad

	lettuce leaves to line four plates
8	ounces baked ham, cut into julienne slices (chicken may be substituted)
2	tablespoons sliced scallions
1	tablespoon spicy hot and sweet mustard
12	fresh asparagus spears, steamed until just tender
1	tablespoon fresh lemon juice
2	teaspoons walnut oil
2	fresh oranges, peeled, halved and thinly sliced
¾	cup Basic Vinaigrette (see Index)
4	ounces feta cheese, crumbled
⅓	cup plain yogurt
½	teaspoon oregano

Toss ham with scallions and mustard and place on lettuce leaves. Toss asparagus with lemon and oil, and place three spears on each salad. Using a fan design, attractively arrange orange slices on ham salad plates. Beat together vinaigrette, feta cheese, yogurt and oregano and spoon over salads.

Key Ingredient: Sausage   Course: Main
Servings: Four   Food Group: Vegetable
Cuisine: American   Temperatures: Cold, room
Meals: Picnic, lunch, dinner   Time: 30 minutes

Picnic Fare Salad

The flavor of this salad is enhanced when it is chilled overnight, but it is also delicious served slightly warm. It's the perfect entrée for your picnic basket. Take along some flavorful cheeses, breads, fresh fruits and hearty beer.

1   pound smoked Kielbasa sausage, simmered
       15 minutes in water and sliced
4   potatoes, scrubbed, thinly sliced and blanched
       7 minutes in Kielbasa water
3   scallions, cleaned and thinly sliced
     cherry tomatoes, halved
2   hard-boiled eggs, peeled and coarsely
       chopped

Dressing:

¼   cup spicy hot and sweet mustard
2   teaspoons toasted sesame seeds
     pinch thyme leaves
     pinch sage (fresh, if available)
¼   cup red wine vinegar
2   cloves garlic, minced
     salt and freshly ground pepper to taste
½   cup olive oil

Drain sausage and potatoes. Combine sausage, crunchy cooked potatoes, scallions, eggs and tomatoes.

Mix dressing and toss with salad. Chill until cool. Serve on a bed of greens.

Key Ingredient: Shrimp   Courses: Main, salad
Servings: Four   Food Group: Seafood, Meat, Vegetable
Cuisine: American   Temperatures: Cold, room
Meals: Lunch, dinner   Time: 1 hour

Cajun Queen Salad

lettuce leaves to line plates, cleaned, dried and torn

8 ounces bottled clam juice

2 cups chicken stock

1 bay leaf

8 ounces shrimp

1½ cups rice

6 ounces ham, cut into julienne strips

½ medium purple onion, minced

½ green pepper, diced

½ red pepper, diced

dash cayenne

dash salt

3 tablespoons olive oil

2 tablespoons spicy hot and sweet mustard

1 clove fresh garlic, pressed

Dressing:

1 tablespoon Dijon-style mustard

1 tablespoon tomato purée

few dashes tabasco sauce

salt

1 teaspoon horseradish

4 tablespoons red wine vinegar

½ cup vegetable oil

pickled okra

Heat clam juice, chicken stock and bay leaf until boiling. Drop in shrimp and cook until just pink. Remove, cool, and peel. Add rice to liquids, cover, and simmer 20 minutes. Turn into mixing bowl and cool to room temperature.

Add ham, shrimp, onion, green and red peppers and cayenne. Toss with olive oil, mustard, garlic and salt to taste.

34

Make dressing in a separate small bowl. Mix mustard, tomato purée, tabasco, horseradish and vinegar. Slowly whisk in oil.

Place salad on torn lettuce leaves. Garnish with pickled okra. Serve with dressing on the side.

Key Ingredient: Turkey	Courses: Main, salad
Servings: Four	Food Group: Poultry, Vegetable
Cuisine: French	Temperatures: Cold, room
Meals: Lunch, dinner, picnic	Time: 30 minutes

French Summer Salad

	spinach leaves, fresh washed and dried
3	potatoes, skins left on, diced
8	ounces smoked turkey, shredded
1	10-ounce package petite peas, slightly blanched
1	large carrot, cleaned and grated
1	small purple onion, very thinly sliced
1	teaspoon tarragon
½	cup sour cream
2	tablespoons Dijon-style mustard
1	clove fresh garlic, pressed
½	teaspoon freshly ground pepper
	salt to taste
3	tablespoons Calvados, or apple brandy

Poach potatoes in chicken stock until crunchy. Combine potatoes, turkey, peas, onion, salt and pepper. Mix tarragon, sour cream, mustard, garlic and Calvados. Toss with salad, and place mixture on plates lined with spinach leaves.

Key Ingredient: Chicken   Course: Salad
Servings: Four   Food Group: Poultry, Pasta
Cuisine: Chinese   Temperature: Cold
Meals: Brunch, lunch   Time: 30 minutes

Hakka Chicken Salad

A group of family and friends became so addicted to Hakka Chicken Salad that they hid the leftovers in my refrigerator for their private and joyous consumption. The other "Hakka" addicts caught them!

1   pound spaghetti or pasta of choice, cooked, drained and slightly warm
1   cup diced or chopped peanuts
1   bunch scallions, thinly sliced
4   stalks celery, diced
     water chestnuts, sliced
1   cooked chicken, picked and shredded
     Napa cabbage or the greens of your choice
     Mandarin oranges and fresh coriander (optional garnish)

Dressing—purée:
4   tablespoons dark Oriental (only) sesame oil
2   tablespoons lemon juice
1   inch fresh ginger root
3   cloves fresh minced garlic
½   cup peanut butter
¼   cup soy sauce or tamari
3   tablespoons spicy hot and sweet mustard
1   teaspoon poppy seeds
     cayenne pepper to taste
     chicken stock, added to desired thickness (½ to 1 cup)
1   cup mayonnaise

After puréeing dressing, add mayonnaise until dressing is creamy but pourable. (Noodles will absorb most of it.) Chill dressing.

Mix chicken, peanuts, scallions, celery and water chestnuts together in a glass or stainless steel bowl. Add dressing and noodles, toss well, and chill.

Serve over thinly shredded Napa cabbage or the greens of your choice. Mandarin oranges and fresh coriander (cilantro) make a nice garnish.

Key Ingredient: Poultry   Course: Main
Servings: Four   Food Group: Poultry
Cuisine: Moroccan   Temperature: Cold
Meals: Lunch, dinner   Time: 30 minutes

Moroccan Poultry Salad

Makes a fabulous filling for hollowed rolls or a topping for a bed of fresh greens.

4	cups cooked and picked chicken (or turkey)
1	cup celery, thinly sliced
½	cup pecans, toasted
3	tablespoons fruity chutney
1	tablespoon spicy hot and sweet mustard
¼	cup scallions, sliced
½	cup mayonnaise
½	cup heavy cream, whipped
	salt and pepper to taste

Combine all ingredients except whipped cream. Chill and, when ready to serve, fold in whipped cream.

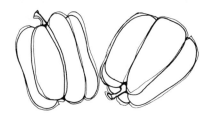

Key Ingredient: Chicken   Courses: Main, salad
Servings: Four to six   Food Group: Poultry, Vegetable, Fruit
Cuisine: American   Temperatures: Cold, room
Meals: Brunch, lunch, picnic   Time: 30 minutes

The Islands Salad

2   cups cooked chicken, shredded

2   cups fresh pineapple, cut into chunks

1   small can water chestnuts, drained, sliced and chilled in ice water

2   medium stalks celery, sliced in thin diagonals and chilled in ice water

2   shallots, minced

   Napa or Oriental cabbage, finely shredded

   Oriental bean sprouts, crisped in ice water

   fresh papaya slices

Dressing:

½   cup spicy hot and sweet mustard

1   teaspoon chives

2   tablespoons capers

2   tablespoons lime juice

1   tablespoon sherry

½   cup mayonnaise

½   cup sour cream

Drain celery and water chestnuts and blot dry. Toss first five ingredients together.
Combine dressing ingredients and pour half over chicken mix. Toss.
Toss cabbage and bean sprouts and line platter. Top with chicken salad. Place papaya slices around sides and drizzle with remaining dressing.

Key Ingredient: Shrimp   Course: Salad
Servings: Four   Food Group: Seafood
Cuisine: Swiss   Temperature: Cold
Meals: Brunch, lunch   Time: 30 minutes

Lugano Salad

tossed greens

two potatoes, sliced into thin rounds

Vinaigrette:

1   tablespoon lemon juice

3   tablespoons red wine vinegar

1   clove fresh garlic, pressed

   salt and pepper to taste

½   cup vegetable oil

Mix all ingredients except oil in a non-aluminum bowl. Slowly drizzle in oil while beating vigorously with a wire whisk.

Shrimp mixture:

1   cucumber, peeled and sliced into thin rounds

6   ounces cooked shrimp

4   ounces mushrooms, sliced and quickly sautéed

½   medium red onion, sliced as thinly as possible

1   hard-boiled egg, grated (for garnish)

Dressing:

2   tablespoons Dijon-style mustard

¼   cup wine vinegar

1   tablespoon sugar

½   cup sour cream

   salt and pepper

1   teaspoon dill, fresh if possible

Prepare potatoes. Blanch potato slices in boiling water for 3 minutes or until cooked but crunchy. Drain and toss with vinaigrette.

Prepare shrimp mixture. Toss ingredients with sour cream dressing.

To assemble, line plates with greens. Arrange crunchy marinated potatoes over greens. Top with shrimp mixture. Garnish with grated hard-boiled egg.

Key Ingredient: Sweet potatoes
Servings: Four
Cuisine: American
Meal: Lunch

Courses: Main, salad
Food Group: Vegetable, Meat
Temperature: Cold
Time: 1 hour

Low Country Salad

Time does not include time needed for refrigeration. Parts of the coastal plains of North Carolina and South Carolina are known as the Low Country. This salad incorporates some of the finest products indigenous to the region.

4	sweet potatoes, cut into matchsticks
1½	cups apple cider
8	ounces Virginia ham, julienned
1	cup toasted pecan halves
4	scallions, chopped
1	bunch parsley, stemmed and chopped
	fresh spinach leaves, washed and stemmed
1	tablespoon Dijon-style mustard
1	teaspoon dill weed
1	tablespoon sherry
1	tablespoon lemon juice
¼	cup remaining apple cider (after poaching sweet potatoes)
2	tablespoons vegetable oil

Heat apple cider in saucepan over medium high heat. Poach sweet potato matchsticks in cider until tender but still crunchy. Cool to room temperature.

Make dressing by mixing mustard, dill, sherry, lemon juice and ¼ cup cider left after poaching. Whisk in oil.

Toss sweet potato matchsticks in dressing and refrigerate until cold. Add ham, scallions and pecans.

Toss spinach leaves and parsley with a bit of dressing. Line plates with greens. Top with salad mixture and drizzle with additional dressing.

Key Ingredients: Tuna and rice
Servings: Four to six
Cuisine: Italian
Meals: Brunch, lunch, dinner

Course: Main
Food Group: Fish, Rice, Vegetable
Temperature: Cold
Time: 20 minutes

Italian Country Salad

This is an especially nice salad for the summer months when fresh basil and Italian plum tomatoes are in abundance.

4   cups cooked rice, warm
2   tablespoons capers
1   6½-ounce can white tuna in oil, drained
½   cup Italian olives, drained of oil
2   tablespoons chopped dried Italian tomatoes
2   tablespoons minced purple onions, plus
       paper-thin rings for garnish

Dressing:
2   tablespoons Dijon-style mustard
2   teaspoons basil, fresh if possible
3   tablespoons balsamic vinegar
2   cloves garlic, minced
½   cup extra virgin olive oil
4   fresh Italian plum tomatoes, washed and
       quartered
     flat Italian parsley sprigs
     lettuce to line plates

Mix dressing and pour over rice in mixing bowl. Add capers, tuna, olives, dried tomatoes and minced onions. Chill slightly. Toss.

Line plates with lettuce leaves. Mound rice salad and top with plum tomato wedges, onion rings and parsley.

Key Ingredient: Gruyère cheese
Servings: Four to six
Cuisine: American
Meals: Lunch, dinner

Courses: Main, salad
Food Group: Dairy, Vegetable
Temperatures: Room, cold
Time: 10 minutes

Gruyère Salad

Simple but wonderful.

8   ounces Gruyère cheese, sliced into matchsticks
4   scallions, cleaned and thinly sliced
2   stalks celery, sliced thinly on the diagonal
8   ounces mushrooms, wiped clean and sliced
½   cup fresh parsley, chopped
¼   cup spicy hot and sweet mustard
2   tablespoons toasted sesame seeds
1   clove garlic, minced
¾   teaspoon freshly ground pepper
¼   cup apple cider vinegar
2   tablespoons oil

Toss all ingredients together.

One who can "cut the mustard" is one who excels at his task. . . .
—an early American expression.

Key Ingredient: Spinach
Servings: Four
Cuisine: Italian
Meals: Brunch, lunch, dinner

Courses: First, Main
Food Group: Vegetable
Temperature: Cold
Time: 30 minutes

Spinach Caesar Salad

8–10 ounces fresh spinach leaves, cleaned, dried and stemmed

1   egg yolk

½   teaspoon anchovy paste

2   cloves fresh garlic, pressed

2   teaspoons Dijon-style, coarse-grain mustard

½   teaspoon Worcestershire sauce

    freshly ground pepper

¼   cup olive oil

¼   cup vegetable oil

½   cup Parmesan cheese, freshly grated

2   tablespoons freshly squeezed lemon juice

Homemade bread cubes:

    bread, crusts removed, cut into ½-inch cubes, enough to equal 1 cup

1   clove fresh garlic, pressed

¼   cup olive oil

Preheat oven to 300°. Place bread cubes on a flat baking sheet. Combine garlic and oil and drizzle over bread cubes while tossing to coat evenly. Bake in preheated oven, tossing occasionally, until crisp, about 30 to 40 minutes.

In large salad bowl, place egg yolk, anchovy paste, garlic, mustard, Worcestershire sauce and pepper. Beat vigorously with a whisk. Very slowly whisk in oils until thick and creamy.

Add spinach and toss until well coated. Add half of cheese and half of croutons. Toss well. Drizzle with lemon juice and gently toss again.

Divide salad onto four chilled salad plates. Top with remaining croutons and cheese.

Key Ingredient: Hearts of palm
Servings: Four
Cuisine: American
Meals: Lunch, dinner

Course: Salad
Food Group: Vegetable
Temperature: Cold
Time: 1 hour

Palm Heart Salad

Time includes marination time.

1   can hearts of palm, drained and chilled
16   large spinach leaves, washed, stemmed and dried
8   pimento strips
1   hard-boiled egg, finely grated

Vinaigrette:

2   tablespoons red wine or balsamic vinegar

1   teaspoon lemon juice

2   tablespoons water

1   teaspoon Dijon-style mustard

1   clove garlic, minced

     pinch each of basil, oregano, salt, pepper
      and thyme

½   cup olive oil

For vinaigrette, combine first six ingredients and whisk. While still whisking, gradually pour in a thin stream of olive oil.

Toss hearts of palm in half of vinaigrette and marinate for one hour. Line four salad plates with spinach leaves. Top with hearts of palm. Garnish with two pimento strips per salad and finely grated egg. Drizzle more vinaigrette over top.

Key Ingredient: Lentils   Course: Salad
Servings: Two   Food Group: Legume
Cuisine: American   Temperature: Cold
Meals: Lunch, dinner   Time: 45 minutes

Tunisian Salad

This contemporary dish is influenced by the small northwestern African country of Tunisia, where lentils are a staple of the diet.

1½   cups lentils, washed
3   cups chicken stock

Dressing:

2   tablespoons red wine vinegar
⅓   cup spicy hot and sweet mustard
3   tablespoons orange juice
1   clove garlic, minced
½   teaspoon oregano leaf
½   cup raisins
2   scallions, thinly sliced
2   oranges, peeled, halved and thinly sliced into
     half moons
2   hard-boiled eggs, peeled and grated
     Boston lettuce, to line plates

Bring chicken stock and lentils to a boil and cook 25 minutes.
Make dressing by combining vinegar, mustard, orange juice, garlic and oregano.
Drain lentils and toss to coat with salad dressing. Add raisins and scallions. Refrigerate until cool.
Mound lentil salad on lettuce leaves. Place overlapping orange slices around perimeter. Top with grated egg.

Key Ingredient: Tomato   Course: Salad
Servings: Four   Food Group: Vegetable, Dairy
Cuisine: American   Temperature: Cold
Meals: Brunch, lunch   Time: 30 minutes

Zesty Campania Salad

2   large fresh tomatoes, sliced

1   8-ounce round mozzarella, sliced into rounds

1   small sweet purple onion, peeled and sliced into paper-thin rounds

2   tablespoons fresh chopped parsley

2   tablespoons Dijon-style mustard

1   clove fresh garlic, pressed

1   tablespoon red wine vinegar

1   tablespoon olive oil

2   teaspoons capers

Alternate slices of tomato, cheese and onion, overlapping to form an attractive arrangement. Repeat this order until all of these three items have been used. Combine next six ingredients and drizzle over salad arrangement. Chill until ready to serve.

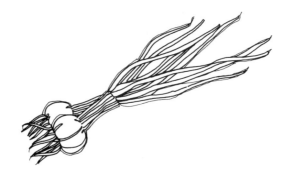

Key Ingredient: Artichokes
Servings: Six
Cuisine: Jewish
Meals: Brunch, lunch

Course: Salad
Food Group: Vegetable
Temperature: Cold
Time: 30 minutes

Sunchoke Salad

1   pound sunchokes (Jerusalem artichokes),
    scrubbed and sliced very thinly
1   bunch scallions, cleaned and chopped
2   fresh tomatoes, cut into ½-inch dices
1   bunch fresh parsley, chopped fine

Dressing:

3   tablespoons fresh lemon juice
2   tablespoons red wine vinegar
    dash salt
1   clove fresh garlic, pressed
2   tablespoons spicy hot and sweet mustard
½   teaspoon basil, fresh if possible, chopped
1   teaspoon anchovy paste
¾   cup vegetable oil

Combine first four ingredients and toss. In a separate bowl, combine next seven ingredients. Gradually pour in oil in a thin stream while whisking vigorously. Pour over vegetables, toss and chill.

Key Ingredient: Pasta   Course: Salad
Servings: Six to eight   Food Group: Pasta
Cuisine: American   Temperature: Cold
Meals: Brunch, lunch   Time: 3 hours and 30 minutes

Family Unit Pasta Salad

Time includes at least 3 hours of refrigeration.

1   pound pasta of choice, cooked according to directions

Drain and toss with:

1   cup homemade or high quality vinaigrette (see Index for Basic Vinaigrette)

2   tablespoons spicy hot and sweet mustard

12   oz. baked ham, cut into julienne strips

10   oz. frozen petite peas, slightly blanched

2   fresh tomatoes, peeled, seeded and diced

10   ounces fresh mushrooms, sliced

Toss all ingredients and chill for at least 3 hours.

Tarragon

Key Ingredient: Ham   Courses: Main
Servings: Four   Food Group: Meat, Pasta
Cuisine: American   Temperature: Cold
Meals: Lunch, dinner   Time: 30 minutes

Four Star Ham Salad

8   ounces baked ham, julienned

4   ounces Gruyère cheese, julienned

2   cups cooked and drained pasta (ziti cut)

2   tablespoons fruity chutney

1   cup sour cream

2   teaspoons Dijon-style mustard

2   teaspoons horseradish

8   ounces fresh beets, cooked, drained and
julienned

Toss all ingredients together except beets. Place on a bed of mixed greens. Garnish by placing beets around the sides of the ham salad mound.

Many people believe it was African slaves who first brought mustard seeds to the United States; others believe the Spaniards carried seeds with them in the eighteenth century while adventuring up the California coast. They marked their path by scattering mustard seeds, which took root and later guided missionaries through what was known as "The Mission Trail."

Key Ingredient: Potatoes   Course: Salad
Servings: Six   Food Group: Vegetable
Cuisine: American   Temperature: Room
Meals: Brunch, dinner   Time: 30 minutes

Red Skin Salad

2	pounds red skin potatoes
1	cup vinaigrette salad dressing, homemade or bottled (see Index for Basic Vinaigrette recipe)
1	clove fresh garlic, pressed
1	tablespoon spicy hot and sweet mustard
6	scallions, finely sliced
½	cup fresh parsley, chopped
2	cups broccoli flowerets, blanched but crisp
	salt

Heat three quarts of water to boiling. Leaving skin on, cook potatoes about 12 to 15 minutes until tender but still firm. While potatoes are still warm, slice in half moons. Toss with remaining ingredients. Add salt to taste. Chill.

EGG DISHES

Key Ingredient: Eggs   Course: Main
Servings: Four   Food Group: Eggs
Cuisine: American   Temperature: Hot
Meals: Brunch, lunch   Time: 30 minutes

Robbin's Free Day Eggs

This dish is delicate, elegant, and also very effective as a "comfort food" to soothe the soul and stomach after a stressful day (or night).

8	eggs, beaten
4	tablespoons sweet butter
3	tablespoons heavy cream
2	tablespoons spicy hot and sweet mustard
½	teaspoon dill weed
1	clove fresh garlic, minced
	salt and pepper
	fresh asparagus, steamed (for garnish)

Melt half of butter in heavy saucepan. Add eggs and stir over low heat. When eggs are nearly set, add remaining butter, bit by bit, and continue stirring. Add cream, mustard, dill weed and garlic. Stir and sprinkle with salt and pepper. Serve over toasted English muffins or in ramekins with toasted bread on the side.

Top with asparagus tips.

Key Ingredient: Egg
Servings: Eight
Cuisine: American
Meals: Breakfast, lunch, brunch,
hors d'oeuvre (when cut into pieces)

Courses: Main, hors d'oeuvre
Food Group: Eggs
Temperature: Hot
Time: 45 minutes

Herb Omelet Roulades

8   eggs

1   tablespoon water

1½ teaspoons chopped mixed herbs (basil,
    oregano, thyme), fresh if available.
    If dried herbs are used, reduce
    to 1 tsp. mixed herbs.

1   tablespoon flour

3   tablespoons spicy hot and sweet mustard

2   tablespoons sweet butter

1   pound feta cheese, crumbled

1   very good non-stick omelet pan

    salsa or marinara sauce for topping

Beat eggs well with water, herbs and flour. Heat omelet pan and add a small portion of the 2 tablespoons of butter to grease pan. Pour about ¼ cup of egg mixture in hot omelet pan. Tilt pan to evenly distribute egg. Cook on one side only until firm enough to remove. Place on platter while cooking remaining egg mixture (¼ cup per omelet). Use the rest of the butter, a little at a time, to grease pan.

Place each omelet, cooked side up, on a flat surface. Place one ounce crumbled feta cheese along center. Roll up securely. Repeat with each omelet.

Preheat oven to 375°. Place rolled omelet roulades on a greased flat baking pan. Brush with melted butter and bake for 10 minutes to warm and melt cheese. Do not overbake.

To serve, top with your favorite salsa or marinara sauce.

Key Ingredient: Eggs   Course: Main
Servings: Six   Food Group: Eggs, Vegetables
Cuisine: American   Temperature: Hot
Meals: Lunch, snack, party   Time: 1 hour

Reunion Frittata

This frittata (Italian baked omelet) was created for a spur-of-the-moment reunion breakfast, and my available fresh vegetables were put to use. Be creative; almost any vegetable at hand may be employed.

½ teaspoon Oriental sesame oil
3 tablespoons sweet butter
2 medium crookneck squash, thinly sliced
2 medium onions, diced
2 cloves garlic, minced
1 teaspoon oregano leaf
9 large eggs, beaten
3 tablespoons spicy hot and sweet mustard
½ teaspoon salt
1 cup shredded Swiss cheese

Preheat oven to 375°. Heat oil and butter in a heavy oven proof 10-inch frying pan. Add squash and onions and sauté 10 minutes. Add next five ingredients. Stir and cook over medium heat for 5 minutes. Sprinkle shredded cheese over top and bake in oven for 15 minutes. Reduce heat to 325° and bake 15 more minutes or until center holds its shape but is not dry.

Key Ingredient: Eggs
Servings: Six to eight
Cuisine: American
Meal: Dinner

Course: Side
Food Group: Egg, Vegetable
Temperature: Hot
Time: 45 minutes

Herb Sponge Roll with Fresh Asparagus

1 tablespoon soft butter

6 eggs, separated

2 tablespoons sugar

½ cup hot chicken stock

1¼ cups flour

1½ teaspoons baking powder

¼ teaspoon salt

¼ teaspoon cayenne

⅓ cup chopped fresh parsley

2 teaspoons chervil

2 tablespoons freshly grated Parmesan

12 ounces fresh asparagus

3 tablespoons Dijon-style mustard

hollandaise (see Index for Basic Hollandaise Recipe)

Grease a sheet pan with butter. Line with wax paper and butter that.

Beat egg yolks until creamy and light colored, about 5 minutes. Add sugar while beating. Add chicken stock. Combine dry ingredients and herbs. Fold this into egg yolk mixture. Beat whites until stiff but not dry. Fold into batter. Pour into prepared pan and bake in a 375° preheated oven for about 10 minutes or until cake springs back to the touch. Unmold onto a clean tea towel and roll loosely while warm.

Steam fresh asparagus until tender crisp. Spread mustard on herb roll. Place asparagus on top and roll up. Slice and top with hollandaise.

Key Ingredient: Eggs	Course: Hors d'oeuvre
Servings: Four	Food Group: Eggs
Cuisine: American	Temperature: Cold
Meals: Brunch, picnic	Time: 30 minutes

Bumpy Stuffed Eggs

6   hard-boiled eggs, peeled

2   tablespoons spicy hot and sweet mustard

1   teaspoon poppy seeds

1   teaspoon sesame seeds

5   tablespoons Hellman's or homemade mayonnaise

     salt to taste

2   tablespoons pesto sauce (homemade or can be purchased frozen)

Split eggs lengthwise. Place yolks in small bowl, and reserve whites. Add mustard, poppy seeds, sesame seeds and mayonnaise to yolks and mash until mixed. Add salt if desired. Spoon yolk mixture back into halves of whites. Top with a dollop of pesto sauce. Chill.

Mustard has been used since antiquity as a healer: as an emetic to induce vomiting; as a laxative; as a gargle for sore throats; foot, hand and body baths for congestion; as a poultice for arthritis, neuralgia, rheumatism and chest congestion; and to help reduce the effects of snakebite and of stings by spiders and other nasty bugs. Hippocrates, the father of medicine, prescribed mustard, writing that the seed releases its oil only after soaking in liquid.

Key Ingredient: Eggs	Courses: Hors d'oeuvre, appetizer
Servings: Four to six	Food Group: Egg, Seafood
Cuisine: Italian	Temperature: Room
Meals: Brunch, lunch, dinner	Time: 30 minutes

Uova Tonnato

This dish makes a fine first course or a light lunch entrée. The tonnato sauce is extremely versatile and marries well with many foods, including veal and chicken. Try using it as a dip for seasonal vegetables.

8   hard-boiled eggs (not overcooked), peeled
       and halved

Tonnato sauce:

1   6½-ounce can tuna, packed in oil

2   teaspoons capers

2   tablespoons Dijon-style mustard

1   teaspoon anchovy paste

½   teaspoon basil

2   cloves garlic, minced

2   tablespoons fresh lemon juice

¾   cup extra virgin olive oil

Place first seven ingredients of sauce in a food processor or blender and purée. With motor running, slowly drizzle in olive oil.

Place a bit of sauce on a platter. Place eggs over sauce cut side down. Spoon over additional sauce and garnish with fresh basil leaves if available, or chopped pimento.

SEAFOOD

Key Ingredient: Mussels	Course: Main
Servings: Four	Food Group: Seafood
Cuisine: French	Temperatures: Hot, room
Meal: Dinner	Time: 1 hour and 30 minutes

Moules au Saffron

4	pounds mussels, scrubbed well
2	tablespoons sweet butter
1	onion, minced
1	tablespoon flour
8	ounces heavy cream
2	tablespoons freshly chopped parsley
1	tablespoon spicy hot and sweet mustard
¼	teaspoon chives
	pinch saffron threads, soaking in 1 tablespoon warm mussel liquid
½	teaspoon coriander

In a large stock pan, heat 2 inches of water until boiling. Add mussels, cover, and steam until mussels open. Remove mussels and keep warm. Retain 2 cups mussel liquid and reduce to ½ cup.

Meanwhile, sauté onion in butter. Add flour and whisk. Whisk in cream and season with freshly ground pepper. Add reduced mussel liquid and cook 15 minutes. Add mustard, chives, parsley, saffron (in mussel broth) and coriander.

Serve mussels in cream sauce over rice or pasta. A steamed artichoke makes a lovely accompaniment.

Key Ingredient: Oysters
Servings: Six
Cuisine: American
Meals: Lunch, dinner

Courses: Appetizer, soup
Food Group: Seafood
Temperature: Hot
Time: 30 minutes

Oyster Mussel Milkbath

1   dozen oysters, fresh and shelled or from a jar, drained
1   dozen mussels, fresh and shelled or smoked and canned, drained
3   tablespoons sweet butter
1   onion, peeled and diced
5   freshly ground peppercorns
½   teaspoon salt
2   tablespoons Dijon-style mustard
1   teaspoon basil
1   cup clam juice
2   cups half-and-half
3   tablespoons sherry

Melt butter in a saucepan over medium-high heat. Add onion and sauté 5 minutes. Add peppercorns, salt, mustard and basil, and stir. Add clam juice, bring to a boil, and reduce by ⅓. Add oysters, mussels, sherry and half-and-half, and heat but *do not* boil. Continue to cook until oysters begin to curl around the edges. Individual bowls of soup should be garnished with a few fresh basil leaves.

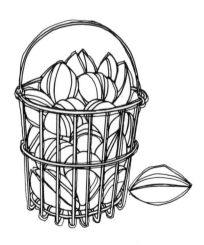

Key Ingredient: Oysters   Course: Main
Servings: Four   Food Group: Seafood
Cuisine: American   Temperature: Hot
Meal: Dinner   Time: 1 hour

Oysters Southport

5	tablespoons sweet butter
⅓	cup parsley, chopped
4	scallions, cleaned and chopped
2	cloves garlic, minced
4	cups fresh spinach
	few dashes cayenne
2	tablespoons spicy hot and sweet mustard
24	oysters, opened on the half shell
	rock salt
¾	cup toasted bread crumbs
2	tablespoons freshly minced parsley
4	tablespoons butter

Melt the 5 tablespoons sweet butter and sauté scallions, parsley and spinach for 8 minutes. Chop very finely or purée in food processor, and add garlic and cayenne.

Place opened oysters on the half shell on a bed of rock salt in a shallow pan. Top each with a dollop of mustard. Top that with spinach mixture.

Melt the 4 tablespoons butter and add bread crumbs. Cook over medium heat until butter is absorbed. Add parsley and stir. Place this mixture on each oyster.

Bake in a preheated 400° oven for 20 minutes.

Key Ingredient: Crab
Servings: Four to six
Cuisine: American
Meals: Appetizer, lunch, dinner

Courses: First, main
Food Group: Seafood
Temperature: Hot
Time: 30 minutes

Middle Sound Cakes of Crab

An English muffin or crumpet ring works beautifully to mold and saute a crab cake. I especially like the presentation of one large crab cake rather than smaller ones.

1   pound lump crabmeat (backfin), drained
1   6-ounce jar marinated artichoke hearts, drained
      and chopped
4   scallions, sliced
½   cup fresh parsley, minced
3   tablespoons mayonnaise
2   tablespoons Dijon-style, coarse-grain mustard
1   tablespoon fresh lemon juice
2   eggs, lightly beaten
3   cups fresh bread cubes, crusts removed and
      cut into ¼-inch cubes
    freshly ground pepper to taste
4   tablespoons unsalted butter (salted will burn)

Combine all ingredients except crab and butter. Gently fold crab into bread mixture without breaking the lumps of meat. Shape into patties of desired size.

In a sauté pan, melt butter over medium-high heat. When butter is hot, place cake in pan and lower heat to medium. Cook crab cake until lightly browned and crisp on each side.

Key Ingredient: Shrimp   Course: Side
Servings: Four   Food Group: Seafood
Cuisine: American   Temperature: Hot
Meals: Dinner, party, picnic   Time: 1 hour

Oak Island Seafood Fritters

4	ounces shrimp, steamed until pink, peeled and chopped coarsely
2	ounces clams (freshly steamed, if possible), drained and chopped
¾	cup yellow corn meal
¾	cup flour
2¼	teaspoons baking powder
½	cup beer
1	large egg
¼	cup celery, finely minced
¼	cup onion, finely minced (Vidalia, if possible)
½	teaspoon salt and freshly ground pepper
1	tablespoon Dijon-style, coarse-grain mustard
	oil for deep frying

Combine dry ingredients. Mix shrimp, clams, beer, egg, vegetables and mustard. Add dry ingredients.

Heat oil in deep saucepan over high heat. Drop fritter batter in by tablespoons, being careful not to crowd. Turn fritters when bottoms become brown. Cook until equally brown on remaining side. Remove, drain on paper towel, and keep warm in low-heat oven. Serve with additional mustard as a dipping sauce.

Seafood

Key Ingredients: Scallops and shrimp   Course: Main
Servings: Four   Food Group: Seafood
Cuisine: American   Temperature: Hot
Meals: Dinner, party, picnic   Time: 30 minutes

Lime and Dill Seafood Skewers

Time does not include 4 to 6 hours for marination.

8   ounces large ocean scallops

8   ounces medium-sized shrimp

8   ounces grouper or halibut filet, cut into
1-inch cubes

⅓   cup fresh lime juice

1   large clove garlic, minced

1   tablespoon Oriental sesame oil

small fresh zucchini, cut into ½-inch slices

fresh button mushrooms

2   ears corn, husked and cut into ½-inch rounds

2   carrots, peeled and cut into ½-inch diagonal slices

2   medium purple onions, peeled and cut into
1/6-inch sections lengthwise so that they are
still attached at the base

2   tablespoons spicy hot and sweet mustard mixed
with 1 teaspoon dill weed

Mix lime juice, fresh garlic and sesame oil. Marinate all the seafood, zucchini, mushrooms and corn rounds in this mixture 4 to 6 hours, turning twice.

Steam carrots and onions over boiling water for 4 minutes.

Assemble food on skewers so that seafoods and vegetables alternate. Make sure foods are securely skewered. (For zucchini, poke skewer through the skin.)

Add 2 tablespoons mustard and dill mixture to marinade juices. Brush over skewers while grilling. Grill over medium-hot barbecue (preferably fruitwood or hardwood) flame for about 8 minutes or until browned on exterior but moist inside.

Serve with additional mustard and dill mixture.

Key Ingredient: Prawns   Course: Main
Servings: Two   Food Group: Seafood
Cuisine: American   Temperature: Hot
Meal: Dinner   Time: 30 minutes

Gently Persuasive Prawns

1	pound raw prawns or shrimp
4	tablespoons sweet butter
2	tablespoons minced shallots
1	clove garlic, minced
⅓	cup Brut champagne
2	teaspoons fresh lemon juice
1	tablespoon spicy hot and sweet mustard
½	teaspoon dill weed
½	tablespoon freshly chopped parsley

Shell and devein prawns. Melt butter in sauté pan over medium-high heat. Add shallots and garlic, and sauté 1 minute. Add prawns and sauté quickly until just pink. Stir in champagne, lemon juice, mustard and dill weed, and simmer 3 minutes. Serve over a bed of hot rice or pasta. Garnish with freshly chopped parsley.

> *More than half the world's supply of mustard is made in Dijon, France. In the eighteenth century, one company in Dijon manufactured more than 90 varieties. Indeed, some in this splendid agricultural area believe that the word* moutarde *comes from the Celtic* moult tarde, *meaning "burn everything." It was a motto of the ancient Dukes of Burgundy.*

Key Ingredient: Prawns   Courses: Main, salad
Servings: Four   Food Group: Seafood
Cuisine: American   Temperature: Cold
Meals: Brunch, lunch, dinner   Time: 30 minutes

Ebbtide Prawns

Boston or Bibb lettuce, cleaned and dried,
  to line plates.

2   pounds prawns, steamed, peeled and deveined
1   ripe avocado, peeled and sliced
2   tablespoons vermouth
¼   cup white wine vinegar
1   tablespoon fresh lemon juice
½   teaspoon anchovy paste
1   clove garlic, minced
3   tablespoons shallots, minced
1½   tablespoons spicy hot and sweet mustard
1   teaspoon poppy seeds
½   teaspoon salt and pepper
¾   cup vegetable oil
¾   cup olive oil

Combine vermouth, vinegar, lemon juice, anchovy paste, garlic, shallots, mustard, poppy seeds, salt and pepper. Whisk. While still whisking, add oils in a steady stream. Alternate prawns and avocado slices on greens. Drizzle dressing over.

Any extra salad dressing may be stored in the refrigerator for up to 3 weeks.

Key Ingredient: Shrimp
Servings: Two
Cuisine: American
Meal: Dinner

Courses: Appetizer, main
Food Group: Seafood
Temperature: Cold
Time: 30 minutes

Drunken Shallot Shrimp

Serves two as an entrée or four as an appetizer.

1   pound fresh shrimp, steamed until just pink,
      deveined and peeled
1   shallot, peeled and minced
1   tablespoon dry vermouth
2   tablespoons fresh lemon juice
1   clove fresh garlic, pressed
½   teaspoon basil
    salt and freshly ground pepper
1   tablespoon Dijon-style mustard
½   cup vegetable oil

Steam shrimp. In a non-aluminum bowl, whisk next seven ingredients together. Very slowly whisk in a thin stream of oil until all is mixed.

Toss the ingredients together and chill. Serve over salad greens of your choice with additional vegetables to garnish or as an appetizer.

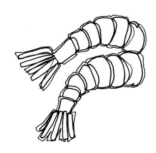

Key Ingredient: Flounder   Course: Main
Servings: Four   Food Group: Seafood
Cuisine: American   Temperature: Hot
Meal: Dinner   Time: 1 hour and 45 minutes

Wrapped Pecan Flounder

Time includes 1 hour of marination.

4	six-ounce filets of flounder (any delicate fish filet may be used)
1	tablespoon spicy hot and sweet mustard, mixed with ½ teaspoon chives
4	tablespoons dry white wine

Marinade:

2	tablespoons lemon juice
1	tablespoon raspberry vinegar or other fruity vinegar
¼	teaspoon tarragon
⅓	cup pecans, chopped very finely
⅓	cup vegetable oil

Garnish:

½	cup pecan halves
8	thin lemon slices

In a stainless-steel or glass pan, spread flounder filets with mustard and chive mixture. Combine ingredients for marinade and pour over filets. Marinate for 1 hour, turning once.

Place each filet on a rectangle of aluminum foil large enough to encase it. Top each marinated filet with another teaspoon of marinade, 2 slices of lemon and ¼ of the pecan halves. Sprinkle with 1 tablespoon dry white wine. Seal foil to envelop fish. Bake in 375° preheated oven for 20 minutes. Place flounder with garnish on individual warmed plates.

Key Ingredient: Fish	Course: Main
Servings: Four	Food Group: Seafood
Cuisine: American	Temperature: Hot
Meal: Dinner	Time: 30 minutes

Fish Filets in Mustard Butter

2   salmon, grouper or swordfish filets

3   tablespoons sweet butter

4   tablespoons shallots, minced

2   tablespoons coarse-grain prepared mustard

½   cup dry white wine

2   tablespoons fresh lime juice, if available

2   tablespoons fresh chopped parsley

1   tablespoon capers

Pat fish filets dry with paper towels. Melt butter over medium-high heat, being careful not to burn. Add fish and cook on each side until browned but just underdone. Place on platter and keep warm in very low-heat oven. Add shallots to sauté pan and brown quickly for 2 minutes. Add rest of ingredients and continue to cook, scraping particles from bottom of pan. Pour over fish filets and sprinkle with more freshly chopped parsley.

Thyme

Key Ingredient: Swordfish   Course: Main
Servings: Four   Food Group: Seafood
Cuisine: American   Temperature: Hot
Meal: Dinner   Time: 1 hour

Swordfish Steaks with Sorrel Hollandaise

4   swordfish or salmon steaks, 6 ounces each
2   tablespoons melted unsalted butter

Quick hollandaise:

3   egg yolks
1   tablespoon lemon juice
1   teaspoon lime juice
1   tablespoon white wine
½   cup butter (1 stick)
    dash cayenne
1   tablespoon spicy hot and sweet mustard
2   tablespoons fresh sorrel, finely chopped (spinach may be used if sorrel is not available)

In blender or food processor fitted with steel blade, place egg yolks, lemon juice, lime juice and white wine. Melt butter until bubbly. Turn on machine and *slowly* pour in butter. Add a dash of cayenne, mustard and sorrel.

Sauté fish steaks in butter, or grill and brush with melted butter while cooking. Top each with hollandaise.

Key Ingredient: Snapper   Course: Main
Servings: Four   Food Group: Seafood
Cuisine: American   Temperature: Hot
Meal: Dinner   Time: ½ hour

Snapper with Lemon Champagne Beurre Blanc

1½   pounds red snapper filets
    salt and pepper
2   tablespoons butter, melted
1   cup dry champagne
1   tablespoon lemon juice
2   teaspoons Dijon-style mustard
¼   teaspoon dill weed
6   tablespoons cold sweet butter

Brush fish with melted butter. Salt and pepper, and bake in a 375° preheated oven for 15 to 20 minutes.

In a saucepan over high heat, reduce champagne and lemon juice to ½ cup. Add mustard and dill weed. Reduce heat. Over very low heat, whisk in 1 tablespoon cold butter until melted. Repeat with each tablespoon of butter. This slow melting of the butter causes the sauce to become creamy. Pour over baked fish and garnish with fresh dill, if available.

Bay Leaves

Key Ingredient: Salmon   Course: Main
Servings: Four   Food Group: Seafood
Cuisine: American   Temperature: Hot
Meals: Brunch, lunch, dinner   Time: 1 hour

Marsha's Salmon Pot Pie

This is the ultimate if fresh salmon is available.

⅓   cup butter

1   cup diced celery

⅓   cup minced onion

6   tablespoons flour

¾   cup clam juice

1⅓   cups milk

⅛ to ¼   teaspoon freshly ground pepper

½   teaspoon salt

⅛   teaspoon paprika

2   tablespoons spicy hot and sweet mustard

1   tablespoon fresh lemon juice

1   tablespoon freshly chopped parsley or chervil

2   teaspoons fresh dill

2   cups fresh baked or poached salmon pieces (leftovers or canned salmon may be substituted)

1   cup sour cream

10   ounces puff pastry, homemade or frozen

    egg wash (1 whole egg beaten with 1 tablespoon milk)

Preheat oven to 450°. Melt butter in saucepan over medium-high heat. When bubbly, add celery and onion and sauté for 5 minutes. Stir in flour and mix well. Slowly pour in clam juice and then milk while stirring constantly. Add salt, pepper, paprika, mustard and lemon juice. Lower heat and cook 15 minutes until thickened. Gently stir in dill, parsley, salmon pieces and sour cream.

Pour salmon mixture into individual gratinée casseroles or into one large casserole.

Cut puff pastry shapes to cover the top of the individual or large baking dishes. Make egg wash by beating egg and milk together. Brush over top of puff pastry.

Reduce oven temperature to 400°. Bake for 20 to 25 minutes or until pastry is puffed and golden.

Key Ingredient: Grouper   Course: Main
Servings: Four   Food Group: Seafood
Cuisine: American   Temperature: Hot
Meal: Dinner   Time: 30 minutes

Sesame Baked Grouper

Grouper, found predominantly in the Southern coastal region, the Caribbean and the Gulf of Mexico, is a fish with delicate white flesh and a taste similar to that of halibut.

2	pounds grouper filets (or other large flesh fish)
	spray shortening
⅓	cup spicy hot and sweet mustard
2	cloves fresh garlic, pressed
2	teaspoons lemon juice
1	tablespoon soy sauce
½	cup (3 ounces) sesame seeds, hulled but not toasted
	lime wedges

Preheat oven to 375°. Blot fish filets with paper towels to dry. Combine mustard, garlic, lemon juice and soy sauce. Spread evenly over fish.

Place sesame seeds on a large plate. Dip each side of prepared filets in sesame seeds, making sure to coat well. Grease pan with spray shortening. Place filets on greased pan and bake for 25 minutes.

Serve with fresh lime wedges.

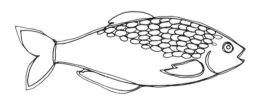

Key Ingredient: Scallops   Course: Main
Servings: Four   Food Group: Seafood
Cuisine: French   Temperature: Hot
Meal: Dinner   Time: 1 hour

Coquilles Saint Jacques en Sauce Champagne au Kiwi

2	tablespoons (¼ stick) unsalted butter
1	large shallot, chopped
1	cup Brut champagne or dry white wine
	salt and freshly ground white pepper
1½	pounds fresh scallops
2	tablespoons spicy hot and sweet mustard
1	teaspoon chives
3	cups whipping cream
¼	cup (½ stick) unsalted butter, cut into pieces
2	kiwi fruit, peeled, sliced ⅛-inch thick (garnish)

Heat 2 tablespoons of butter in large skillet over medium heat. Add shallot and sauté lightly. Add champagne or wine and simmer until reduced by half. Season with salt and white pepper. Add scallops, top with piece of buttered parchment or waxed paper, and simmer gently until just cooked through, about 2 to 3 minutes. Remove scallops with slotted spoon and keep warm.

Increase heat and reduce juices to a glaze. Blend in mustard, chives and cream, and simmer until thickened and mixture lightly coats spoon, about 20 minutes. Whisk in remaining butter. Taste, and adjust seasoning. Divide sauce among warmed dinner plates. Arrange scallops over sauce and top each with a slice of kiwi.

POULTRY

Key Ingredient: Cornish game hen Course: Main
Servings: Six Food Group: Poultry
Cuisine: American Temperature: Hot
Meal: Dinner Time: 1 hour and 30 minutes

Southern Plantation Cornish Game Hen

One pan of Basic Cornbread (see page 85) is used.

6   Cornish game hens

Stuffing:

2   medium onions, diced
2   ribs celery, diced
1   cup fresh figs, chopped (use dried figs if fresh are not in season)
½   cup chopped pecans
6   ounces smoked sausage, diced
4   tablespoons sweet butter
1¼ cups chicken broth
2   tablespoons spicy hot and sweet mustard
1   clove fresh garlic, pressed
2   sage leaves, chopped
⅓   cup sherry
1   Recipe Basic Cornbread, crumbled

Basting mixture:

2   tablespoons spicy hot and sweet mustard
1   clove fresh garlic, pressed
1   tablespoon sherry
2   tablespoons sweet butter, melted
    mixture of 2 tablespoons fresh chopped sage and parsley

Melt 4 tablespoons butter in pan over medium-high heat and sauté onions and celery until onions are translucent. Add pecans and sausage, and cook 5 more minutes. Add this mixture along with figs, broth, mustard, sage, garlic and sherry to one pan crumbled cornbread.

Rinse inside of game hens and salt and pepper. Pack loosely with stuffing. (Remaining stuffing may be baked in a covered casserole or in aluminum foil.) After game hens have been trussed, brush with the combined ingredients for the basting mixture. Bake in a preheated 375° oven for about 50 minutes or until brown. Baste often while baking.

Key Ingredient: Chicken
Servings: Twelve
Cuisine: American
Meals: Brunch, party

Courses: Hors d'oeuvre, appetizer
Food Group: Poultry
Temperature: Cold
Time: 2 hours and 30 minutes

Calvert's Chicken Paté

Time consuming, but worth the effort, for the taste is unusually delicate. Please note that there is no liver used in this paté. The chicken can also be barbecued or smoked to add lots of flavor. If preparation time is dear, the tomato layer may be omitted and the chicken paté alone can be baked for one hour or until firm.

Chicken layer:

3½	pounds chicken breasts and thighs
2	medium onions, diced and sautéed in butter until translucent
2	tablespoons butter
3	eggs
8	ounces whipping cream
3	tablespoons spicy hot and sweet mustard
	salt and pepper to taste
	juice of one lemon
½	teaspoon thyme, fresh if possible
2	cloves garlic, pressed

Tomato layer:

3	fresh medium-sized tomatoes, chopped
1½	cups thick bechamel sauce
2	eggs
¼	teaspoon oregano leaf
1	teaspoon Worcestershire sauce
1	clove garlic, pressed
1	tablespoon tomato purée
4	ounces fresh asparagus, coarse ends snapped off and steamed until crisp

Béchamel Sauce (Classic White Sauce):

2	tablespoons butter
2	tablespoons flour
1	cup milk
	dash each salt, pepper, nutmeg

In saucepan, melt butter over low heat. Whisk in flour. Slowly pour in milk while whisking constantly. Cook and stir sauce until it is thickened and smooth. Add salt, pepper and nutmeg.

Bake chicken uncovered, on a flat baking sheet, 40 minutes in hot oven (400°). While baking, prepare onions.

Skin and bone chicken and place chicken meat in food processor. Place remaining ingredients for chicken layer in food processor until smooth. Pour half of this mixture into a greased bread loaf pan. Set aside mixture in loaf pan and reserve the other half. Wash food processor.

Put all ingredients for tomato layer in food processor and process until smooth. Pour (gently) over chicken mixture in loaf pan. Place asparagus lengthwise in tomato layer only. Gently press so that the asparagus are covered. Paté must now be partially baked until firm enough to support the top layer. Place loaf pan in a larger deep pan, and fill the large pan with hot water until it reaches half the height of the loaf pan. Bake at 375° for 40 minutes or until tomato layer begins to get firm.

Remove paté from oven and quickly spoon remaining chicken mixture over tomato layer. Return to oven to bake about 50 minutes more or until quite firm. Cool and then chill in refrigerator.

Loosen edges by running a knife around the sides. Invert onto a platter and unmold. Garnish with fresh thyme. (Chicken and béchamel sauce may be prepared in advance.)

> *"Mustard . . . is to hot dogs and salad dressing what*
> *ice cream is to a cone and a pickle is to pastrami."*
> —*From the* Food Encyclopedia, *by Craig Claiborne*

Key Ingredient: Chicken   Course: Main
Servings: Eight   Food Group: Poultry
Cuisine: American   Temperature: Hot
Meal: Dinner   Time: 45 minutes

Grilled Orange Chicken Breast with Bacon

Time does not include overnight marination.

8	chicken breasts, unskinned
1	onion, finely chopped
¼	cup fresh orange juice
⅓	cup spicy hot and sweet mustard
1	teaspoon dill weed
3	cloves fresh garlic, pressed
3	tablespoons soy sauce
3	tablespoons white vinegar
	grated rind of one orange
16	slices bacon

Marinate chicken in next eight ingredients overnight. Wrap two slices of bacon around each breast and secure with toothpicks. Grill over medium hot coals for approximately 35 minutes or until moist but firm. Chicken may also be baked in a 375° oven for 40 minutes.

Key Ingredient: Duck   Course: Main
Servings: Two   Food Group: Poultry
Cuisine: American   Temperature: Hot
Meal: Dinner   Time: 3 hours and 30 minutes

Brandied Duck with Olives

1	roasting duckling
1	cup pimento-stuffed green olives, sliced
1½	tablespoons cornstarch, dissolved in 2 tablespoons cold water
1½	cups chicken stock (preferably homemade)
2	tablespoons spicy hot and sweet mustard
2	tablespoons fresh lemon juice
¼	cup brandy

Prick duck all over with a fork. Place on a rack in a roasting pan and bake in a 325° preheated oven for 3 hours. Drain off the fat periodically while baking.

Remove roasted duck from pan and place on platter to keep warm. Remove all fat but 1 tablespoon in roasting pan. Pour any juices, pan scrapings and 1 tablespoon duck fat into saucepan. Whisk in cornstarch mixture over medium heat. Stir until any lumps are removed. Gradually whisk in chicken stock, mustard, lemon juice and brandy. Simmer 20 minutes, stirring often. Add olives and simmer 10 minutes.

Cut duck into pieces and pour some of the olive sauce over them. Serve with additional sauce on the side.

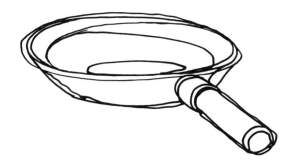

Key Ingredient: Chicken Course: Main
Servings: Four Food Group: Poultry
Cuisine: American Temperature: Hot
Meal: Dinner Time: 1 hour

Chicken Breasts Escoffier Style

4 chicken breast halves, skinned, boned and flattened between sheets of wax paper

2 tablespoons spicy hot and sweet mustard mixed with ½ teaspoon basil

1 cup fresh bread crumbs

1 tablespoon olive oil

4 tablespoons sweet butter (salted butter will burn)

Sauce:

2 tablespoons butter

2 tablespoons flour

1 tablespoon spicy hot and sweet mustard mixed with ½ teaspoon chives

1 teaspoon anchovy paste

¾ cup chicken stock

¾ cup cream

2 tablespoons cognac

1 tablespoon green peppercorns

Blot chicken breasts dry with paper towel. Sprinkle with salt and pepper. Coat with mustard and basil mixture, then dredge in bread crumbs, making sure they are well coated. Chill 20 minutes.

Heat butter and olive oil over medium heat, watching closely to prevent burning. Add breasts and brown on each side. Do not overcook breasts. Place on paper towels and keep warm.

Melt butter in saucepan. Whisk in flour, anchovy paste and mustard and chive mixture. Slowly whisk in stock and cream. Add strained scrapings from sauté pan. Cook over medium heat until sauce thickens, stirring until smooth. Simmer 15 minutes. Add peppercorns. If sauce becomes too thick, thin with additional stock.

Note: Sauce may be made ahead and drippings added.

Key Ingredient: Chicken   Course: Main
Servings: Four   Food Group: Poultry
Cuisine: American   Temperature: Hot
Meals: Lunch, dinner   Time: 45 minutes

Sesame Chick Strips

This dish is a light fare entrée: not only is it not filling, but it is low in calories as well.

4   chicken breasts, boned and flattened between
      two sheets of wax paper

3   tablespoons spicy hot and sweet mustard mixed
      with two cloves fresh garlic, pressed

2   teaspoons tamari or soy sauce

¾   cup hulled sesame seeds

Slice chicken breasts into strips ⅜" wide.
Mix mustard and garlic mixture with tamari.
Toss chicken strips in mustard sauce and then coat with sesame seeds. Grill quickly over barbecue fire.
Note: Chicken strips may be prepared in advance and kept refrigerated.

Key Ingredient: Corn meal   Course: Side
Servings: Eight   Food Group: Grain
Cuisine: American   Temperatures: Hot, room
Meals: Lunch, dinner   Time: 40 minutes

Basic Cornbread

1   cup enriched corn meal

1   cup all-purpose flour

4   teaspoons baking powder

½   teaspoon salt

1   cup milk

1   egg

¼   cup vegetable oil

Heat oven to 425°. Grease an 8-inch square baking pan. Combine dry ingredients. Add milk, egg and oil, and beat about 1 minute or until smooth. Pour into prepared pan. Bake 20 to 25 minutes or until golden brown.

Key Ingredient: Chicken   Course: Main
Servings: Four   Food Group: Poultry
Cuisine: American   Temperature: Hot
Meal: Dinner   Time: 1 hour

Chicken Roulades in Phyllo

4	chicken breast halves, skinned, boned and flattened
1½	tablespoons spicy hot and sweet mustard
3	tablespoons olive oil
¾	cup mushrooms, chopped
⅓	cup onion, finely chopped
2	tablespoons dry sherry
2	ounces hazelnuts, toasted and chopped
2	ounces dried apricots, chopped
	pinch fines herbes
¼	cup fresh bread crumbs
¼	teaspoon salt
1	tablespoon olive oil
4	phyllo pastry leaves
4	tablespoons butter, melted for brushing pastry

Place chicken breasts between two sheets of wax paper and flatten with mallet. Spread with equal portions of mustard.

Heat oil in sauté pan. Add onion and sauté 3 minutes. Add mushrooms and sauté 2 more minutes. Add sherry, nuts, apricots, bread crumbs, herbs and salt. Cook 4 minutes.

Divide this mixture among four breasts. Roll and secure with toothpicks. Heat additional olive oil over high heat. Sear chicken rolls very quickly on all sides. Cool and remove toothpicks. (Breasts should hold the rolled shape.)

Layer two sheets of phyllo and, with a pastry brush, spread with melted butter. Layer two more sheets. Cut layered phyllo rectangles in four equal parts. Place a rolled chicken breast on each square and roll up, tucking in ends and brushing with melted butter. Brush outside of each roll with melted butter.

Bake at 425° for 15 to 20 minutes or until browned.

MEAT

Key Ingredient: Pork Tenderloin   Course: Main
Servings: Six   Food Group: Meat
Cuisine: American   Temperature: Hot
Meal: Dinner   Time: 2 hours

Smoked Pork Tenderloin

Time does not include time needed for marination. I truly believe that some of the finest flavors in food preparation are obtained by the simple processes of marinating and then grilling or smoking. Here's to an abundance of low-cal flavor!

3   pounds boneless pork tenderloin

Marinade:

1   teaspoon salt, freshly ground pepper

1   bay leaf

4   cloves garlic, minced

3   leaves sage (fresh if possible), chopped

3   tablespoons fresh lemon juice

2   tablespoons red wine vinegar

½   cup dry vermouth

½   teaspoon hot chili oil

½   teaspoon Oriental sesame oil

Marinate pork in above ingredients overnight. Reserve marinade for sauce.

Use a grill with a lid and build a small fire with hardwood. (Fruitwood gives an especially nice flavor.) Sear roast until brown. Let fire die down and then continue to grill with lid on. Turn roast occasionally and grill approximately 1 hour (depending on fire) or until just beyond pink in the center.

Place pork on platter and cover with foil to keep warm. Quickly make sauce by bringing marinade to boil in a small, non-aluminum pan. Add ½ cup water and boil 3 minutes. Reduce heat and add:

2   tablespoons spicy hot and sweet coarse-grain mustard

2   tablespoons capers

2   tablespoons fresh parsley, chopped

Lower heat to a simmer and, bit by bit, whisk in 6 tablespoons cold sweet butter. Slice pork and top rounds with sauce.

Key Ingredient: Sausage
Servings: Six
Cuisine: American
Meals: Brunch, lunch, snack

Courses: Appetizer, side
Food Group: Meat
Temperatures: Hot, room
Time: 1 hour and 30 minutes

Southern Wrapped Sausage

1	8-inch Kielbasa sausage
½	cup all-purpose flour
1½	cups yellow corn meal
1	teaspoon salt
2	teaspoons sugar
1	tablespoon baking powder
3	eggs
1¼	cups half-and-half
3	tablespoons vegetable oil
1	medium onion, diced and sautéed in 1 tablespoon sweet butter
1	small can diced green chilies, drained
3	tablespoons spicy hot and sweet mustard

Poach Kielbasa in water for 10 minutes. Set aside. Mix dry ingredients together. In a separate bowl, lightly beat eggs. Add half-and-half, oil, chilies, onion and mustard. Add dry mixture and beat until combined well. Pour half of batter into a greased loaf pan. Lay sausage on top and pour over remaining batter. Bake in a preheated 325° oven for 45 minutes. Let stand 10 minutes, unmold onto a cookie sheet, and turn bottom up. Bake another 10 minutes to brown top. When cool, slice and top with additional mustard. Makes one 8½-by-4¼-inch loaf.

"A tale without love is like beef without mustard; an insipid dish."

—Anatole France

Key Ingredient: Beef   Courses: Appetizer, main
Servings: Two to six   Food Group: Meat
Cuisine: Italian   Temperature: Cold
Meal: Dinner   Time: 1 hour

Carpaccio

These paper-thin slices of raw beef make elegant, melt-in-your-mouth dish as an appetizer or a light entrée.

1	pound beef filet
½	cup extra virgin or very light olive oil
½	cup lemon juice
¼	cup dry red wine
1	tablespoon fresh shallots, minced
2	tablespoons drained capers
2	tablespoons Dijon-style mustard
2	tablespoons fresh chopped parsley
	salt
4	ounces fresh mushrooms, cleaned and sliced
2	tablespoons freshly grated Parmesan cheese

Trim fat from beef, wrap beef in foil, and place in freezer for 30 minutes to facilitate slicing.

While meat is in freezer, make sauce by combining lemon juice, wine, shallots, capers, mustard and parsley. Gradually whisk in olive oil by pouring in a small stream. Add salt and mushrooms and toss. Refrigerate for at least 20 minutes.

Remove meat from freezer and with a very sharp, thin knife slice on a diagonal into paper-thin slices.

Place beef slices on a platter or individual plates. Top with sauce, serving additional sauce on the side. Sprinkle Parmesan cheese over the filet slices.

Key Ingredient: Chuck roast   Course: Main
Servings: Twelve   Food Group: Meat
Cuisine: American   Temperature: Hot
Meals: Lunch, dinner   Time: 10 hours

Nana's Chili

Best if made a day in advance and kept refrigerated to season, this chili takes a bit of effort but is well worth it. Try serving it over rice or in a bowl with diced cheddar cheese floating in it. Part of this batch may be frozen.

4	pounds chuck roast
2	tablespoons vegetable oil
4	tablespoons spicy hot and sweet mustard
4	cups water
2	cups beer (strong dark beer is best)
5¾	cups tomato juice or V8
6	cloves garlic, minced
1	pound dried pinto beans (presoaked at least 8 hours in cold water)
¼	cup olive oil
5	medium onions, diced
2	green peppers, chopped
4	large stalks celery, diced
4	fresh tomatoes, diced
3	tablespoons chili powder
2	teaspoons salt
1	teaspoon ground cumin
2	teaspoons oregano
3	jalapeno peppers, finely chopped (or 1 teaspoon cayenne)

Heat vegetable oil in large heavy kettle until very hot. Sear chuck roast on all sides. Remove from pot and coat with mustard. Return and add garlic and next three liquids. Bring to a boil, then reduce and simmer (no stirring needed) at least 8 hours (or overnight) or until meat falls off the bones. Remove meat from liquid and set aside.

Turn meat liquid to high, add drained pintos, and heat to boiling. Reduce heat to medium high and cook, bubbling gently to reduce liquid, until beans are very tender—about 1½ hours.

Meanwhile, heat olive oil in a separate large sauté pan. Add next four vegetables and sauté over medium-high heat for 10 minutes. Add spices and cook 3 more minutes.

Add this mixture to the pot of cooking beans.

Shred beef and discard bones and fat. Add to bean and vegetable mixture after beans have cooked one hour.

Adjust seasoning to your liking.

Key Ingredient: Ground round   Course: Main
Serving: One   Food Group: Meat
Cuisine: American   Temperature: Hot
Meals: Lunch, dinner   Time: 15 minutes

Daddy Burt's Pocket Burgers

If you think this recipe is just for an ordinary hamburger in pocket bread, read on! There is a little treasure in every burger. Proportions are given per burger so you may adapt this to as many servings as you like.

8   ounces ground round

1   teaspoon capers, chopped

1   tablespoon onion, finely minced

1   teaspoon spicy hot and sweet mustard

4   teaspoons Parmesan, freshly grated

For each burger, start by dividing the eight ounces of ground round into two equal, flat, round patties. On first patty, sprinkle half of grated Parmesan.

Mix capers, onion and mustard together. Spoon this mixture on top of cheese, being careful to keep near center of burger. Top with remaining 2 teaspoons of cheese.

Place remaining ground round patty on top and press two patties together very firmly around edges. Make sure filling is firmly encased.

Burgers may be cooked on a stove top grill, seared in a hot, heavy skillet, broiled or grilled over charcoal. For broiling or grilling, allow 3 to 4 minutes per side for medium rare.

Key Ingredient: Lamb
Servings: 4 (or 32, if used
as an hors d'oeuvre)
Cuisine: American
Meals: Lunch, dinner, hors d'oeuvre

Courses: Appetizer, first, main
Food Group: Meat
Temperature: Hot
Time: 30 minutes

Lamb Burgers with Caesar Mayonnaise

This makes a fine hors d'oeuvre if you make small lamb balls and sauté them individually. Garnish with spinach and smaller tomato wedges, and use the Caesar Mayonnaise as a dipping sauce.

2   pounds ground lamb
½   cup freshly chopped parsley
3   scallions, cleaned and very thinly sliced
2   teaspoons Dijon-style mustard
½   teaspoon salt
½   teaspoon freshly cracked pepper
4   ounces fresh spinach leaves, cleaned, dried, stemmed
4   large slices fresh tomato
    Caesar Mayonnaise

Make mayonnaise first, with recipe below.

Break lamb into bowl and mix with parsley, scallions, mustard, salt and pepper. Form into four patties.

Heat large, heavy skillet over medium-high heat until hot. Add lamb patties, and sear 2 minutes on each side. Reduce heat to medium and cook 2 more minutes per side. The lamb burgers will be medium rare. Place momentarily on paper towels to drain excess grease.

Line four plates with fresh spinach leaves. Top spinach with hot lamb burger. Top with tomato slice and add a dollop of Caesar Mayonnaise.

Caesar Mayonnaise:
2   cloves fresh garlic, peeled
2   egg yolks
2   teaspoons spicy hot and sweet mustard
2   tablespoons freshly grated Parmesan cheese
1   teaspoon Worcestershire sauce
1   anchovy filet
1½ tablespoons fresh lemon juice

¼ teaspoon freshly ground pepper

¾ cup olive oil

1 cup vegetable oil

In food processor or blender, place garlic, egg yolks, mustard, Worcestershire, anchovy, lemon juice and pepper. Process until creamy. Slowly drizzle in olive oil and then vegetable oil. If mayonnaise becomes too thick, a tablespoon or two of water may be added.

Yields 1¾ cups.

Key Ingredient: Veal	Course: Main
Servings: Four	Food Group: Meat
Cuisine: French	Temperature: Hot
Meal: Dinner	Time: 30 minutes

Veal Gorgonzola

8 veal scallops, each flattened between two sheets of wax paper

4 tablespoons sweet butter

2 tablespoons spicy hot and sweet mustard, mixed with ½ teaspoon basil

juice of one lemon

¼ cup dry white wine

4 ounces Gorgonzola cheese

Melt butter in sauté pan until sizzling. Sear one side of each veal scallop and remove to platter. Drizzle the cooked side of each veal scallop with lemon juice. Spread each with an equal portion of mustard and basil mixture and top each with ⅛ crumbled Gorgonzola.

At this time, preheat broiler unit of oven. Carefully return veal to sauté pan and sauté uncooked side for 2 minutes.

Spoon butter scrapings from pan over cheese and dash with white wine. Place under broiler briefly, just until cheese melts. Serve topped with pan juices.

Key Ingredient: Lamb   Course: Main
Servings: Four   Food Group: Meat
Cuisine: American   Temperature: Hot
Meal: Dinner   Time: 2 hours

Proffitt's Lamb Leg (Stuffed and Smoked)

Time does not include overnight marination. This masterpiece always draws raves and cries for an encore. If you have any remains, your guests may stay on just to partake of the outstanding sandwiches.

5   pound leg of lamb, butterflied and pounded 1 inch thick

Marinade:

⅔   cup dry red wine

2   tablespoons fresh lemon juice

½   cup olive oil

2   tablespoons Dijon-style mustard

1   teaspoon basil

Filling:

1   pound ricotta cheese

2   10-ounce packages frozen chopped spinach, thawed and squeezed dry

6   scallions, chopped

1   egg, beaten

1   cup pine nuts

1   teaspoon oregano

Coating:

½   cup spicy hot and sweet mustard

3   teaspoons anchovy paste

2   cloves garlic, minced

Marinate leg of lamb overnight.

Make filling by combining the next six ingredients and mixing well.

Spread inside of flattened lamb leg with filling, keeping it in the center. Roll the lamb around stuffing and tie with twine at 1½-inch intervals.

For smoking, use a grill with a cover. Use hardwood or mesquite as fuel. Build a hot fire that is no longer flaming. Sear lamb until brown on all sides. Place lamb on platter until fire cools slightly, and spread with coating. More coating should be brushed on during smoking. Add lamb, and smoke for approximately 1 hour with cover on, turning often. Test lamb for doneness (should be pink). Let stand 10 minutes before removing string and slicing into filled rounds.

Key Ingredient: Veal   Course: Main
Servings: Four   Food Group: Meat
Cuisine: American   Temperature: Hot
Meal: Dinner   Time: 30 minutes

Veal with Cognac and Mustard

8	veal scallopine, pounded ¼-inch thick
	salt and pepper, freshly ground
	flour
2	teaspoons mustard powder
2	tablespoons sweet butter
2	tablespoons olive oil
¼	teaspoon freshly chopped shallots
8	ounces heavy cream
3	tablespoons cognac or brandy
2	tablespoons spicy hot and sweet mustard
1	tablespoon freshly grated lemon rind

Mix flour, mustard powder, salt and pepper. Dredge veal slices in this mixture and pat off excess. Heat butter and oil in a heavy skillet over high heat. Sauté veal very quickly—a minute on each side. Place veal on serving platter and keep warm. Turn heat to medium, and scrape all the particles left in pan. Add shallots and brown quickly, about 2 minutes. Deglaze pan with cognac, and add heavy cream. Bring to a boil, and reduce for 5 minutes. Add mustard and lemon rind. Spoon sauce over veal to serve.

Key Ingredient: Pork   Course: Main
Servings: Four   Food Group: Meat
Cuisine: Tex Mex   Temperature: Hot
Meals: Lunch, dinner   Time: 45 minutes

Country Style Pork Ribs with Tequila Sauce

This sauce has a variety of uses. It works very well with grilled chicken or even fish. As a dipping sauce, try it with raw or steamed vegetables. Great with "skin on" potatoes, cooked until just tender.

3½   pounds meaty country-style pork ribs
4   tablespoons spicy hot and sweet mustard
   tequila sauce (recipe follows)
   fresh cilantro

Preheat oven to 400°. Coat each rib with mustard. Place ribs on rack in shallow baking pan and bake for 30 minutes. While meat is baking, prepare Tequila Sauce:

1   4-ounce jar whole pimentos
1   egg yolk
2   tablespoons fresh lemon juice
2   cloves garlic, peeled
1   teaspoon Dijon-style mustard
2   tablespoons golden tequila
   dash tabasco
⅓   cup roasted pepitas (pumpkin seeds)
¼   teaspoon salt
¾   cup vegetable oil

Place pimentos, egg yolk, lemon juice, garlic, tequila, tabasco and salt in a food processor or blender. While processing to a purée, slowly pour in oil. Process until creamy.
Top baked ribs with Tequila Sauce and garnish with fresh cilantro.

"Mustards ain't no good without roast beef," according to Chico Marx.

PASTA

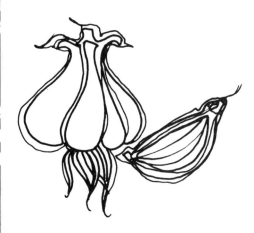

Key Ingredient: Pasta   Course: Main
Servings: Four   Food Group: Pasta
Cuisine: Contemporary Italian   Temperature: Hot
Meals: Lunch, dinner   Time: 45 minutes

Dorothea's Mostaciolli

2   tablespoons sweet butter
1   tablespoon flour
1   cup half-and-half
    dash cayenne, nutmeg, salt and pepper
1   tablespoon Dijon-style mustard
1   fresh clove garlic, pressed
    grated rind of one lemon
¾   cup chopped toasted almonds
2   cups fresh spinach, steamed until wilted, chopped
1   pound mostaciolli pasta
    juice of one lemon

Melt butter in saucepan over medium heat. Whisk in flour. Gradually whisk in half-and-half until smooth, and add spices, mustard, garlic and lemon rind. Simmer for 20 minutes or until slightly thickened.

Meanwhile, bring pasta water to a boil and cook according to directions. Drain and toss with fresh lemon juice.

Add nuts and spinach to cream sauce and toss with mostaciolli.

Key Ingredient: Pasta   Course: Main
Servings: Four   Food Group: Pasta
Cuisine: Contemporary Italian   Temperature: Hot
Meals: Lunch, dinner   Time: 30 minutes

Asparagus Tip Pasta

1	pound fusilli pasta (spirals)
3	tablespoons olive oil
4	tablespoons sweet butter
10	ounces fresh asparagus tips (1-inch lengths)
1	cup pitted black olives, sliced
3	tablespoons spicy hot and sweet mustard
2	teaspoons poppy seeds
2	tablespoons fresh lemon juice
½	cup Kasseri cheese (or fresh Parmesan), finely grated
	salt and freshly cracked black pepper

Cook pasta according to directions. While pasta is cooking, melt butter in sauté pan over medium-high heat. Add asparagus tips to butter and cook briefly about 4 minutes.

Drain pasta and toss with olive oil. Add asparagus tips, butter, olives, mustard, poppy seeds, lemon juice, salt and pepper. Top with freshly grated cheese.

Key Ingredient: Spaghetti Courses: Main, side
Servings: Four to six Food Group: Pasta
Cuisine: Italian Temperature: Hot
Meals: Lunch, dinner Time: 30 minutes

White Cloud Pasta

1	pound very thin spaghetti
2	cups heavy cream
½	teaspoon rosemary, finely crushed
2	cloves fresh garlic, minced
1½	tablespoons Dijon-style mustard
½	teaspoon basil
6	ounces diced Fontina cheese
1	cup toasted walnuts, chopped

Bring 4 quarts salted water to a boil in a large pot. In a separate saucepan, heat cream, rosemary, garlic, mustard and basil to the boiling point. Simmer while cooking pasta. Cook pasta until al dente, drain, and return to pot. Pour cream sauce over, add Fontina and walnuts, and toss well. When serving, top with freshly ground pepper.

Mustard seed is a symbol of fertility for ancient Hindus.

Key Ingredient: Pasta   Course: Main
Servings: Four   Food Group: Pasta
Cuisine: Italian   Temperature: Hot
Meals: Breakfast, lunch, dinner   Time: 45 minutes

Ricotta and Vegetable Matchstick Pasta

1   pound pasta, angel hair if available
2   medium carrots, scrubbed and cut into matchstick size
2   medium crookneck squash, cut into matchstick size
4   scallions, chopped
2   tablespoons olive oil
2   leeks, cleaned and sliced
2   tablespoons Dijon-style, coarse-grain mustard
1   clove fresh garlic, pressed
6   ounces ricotta cheese
2   cups half-and-half
6   tablespoons butter
    freshly grated Parmesan cheese

Heat olive oil and sauté carrots and leeks over medium heat for 5 minutes. Add squash and scallions and sauté for 3 minutes more.

Cook pasta until al dente. Drain and return to pot. Toss butter with warm, drained pasta. Toss with ricotta cheese, half-and-half, mustard, garlic and sauteéd vegetables. Heat quickly to warm. Serve topped with freshly grated Parmesan.

VEGETABLE DISHES

Key Ingredients: Turnips, smoked fish
and Chèvre cheese
Servings: Six to eight
Cuisine: American
Meals: Appetizer, lunch, dinner

Courses: First, main
Food Group: Vegetable, Seafood
Temperature: Warm
Time: 45 minutes

Turnip Latkes with
Smoked Trout and Chèvre

The latkes, which are the most time-consuming components of the recipe, may be made in advance and kept refrigerated or frozen. To prepare, thaw and then warm slightly in a 350° oven.

4   medium size turnips, peeled and grated
      to equal 3 cups

1   cup grated apple

1   medium onion, minced

¼   cup flour

¼   teaspoon salt, pepper to taste

2   tablespoons spicy hot and sweet mustard

2   eggs

1   teaspoon dill weed

¼   cup oil

3   ounces cream cheese, softened

3   ounces Chèvre (goat's cheese)

4   ounces smoked trout or smoked salmon

3   scallions, cleaned and finely sliced

Mix grated turnips, grated apple, minced onion, flour, salt, pepper and dill. Beat eggs with mustard and add to turnip mixture. Combine well.

In a large heavy skillet, heat oil over medium heat until hot. For each latke, drop a heaping tablespoonful of mixture into oil. Flatten slightly with spoon. Cook on first side 3 to 4 minutes or until browned. Flip and cook 3 minutes on other side. Drain on paper towels, then place on warmed platter while cooking the rest of the latkes. (Recipe yields 18 latkes.)

Mix Chèvre and cream cheese together until well combined. Place an equal portion of cheese mixture on top of each latke. Top cheese with equal strips of smoked fish. Top with sliced scallions and place on warmed platter. Serve while still warm.

Key Ingredient: Mustard
Servings: Yields 3 cups
Cuisine: American
Meals: Topping, dressing, dip

Courses: Salad, hors d'oeuvre
Food Group: Vegetable
Temperature: Cold
Time: 5 minutes

Rita's Rowdy Salad Dressing

⅓   cup red wine vinegar
¾   cup spicy hot and sweet mustard
1   cup vegetable oil
    dash cayenne
1   teaspoon salt
2½   cups half-and-half
2   tablespoons toasted sesame seeds
1   tablespoon poppy seeds

Place vinegar, mustard and cayenne in blender or food processor. While processing, slowly pour in oil. Add salt and then slowly pour in half-and-half. Add seeds last and mix well but do not crush seeds.

Aside from traditional uses, this is great on seafood and on salmon and tuna salads.

Key Ingredient: Vegetables   Course: Side
Servings: Five   Food Group: Vegetable
Cuisine: American   Temperature: Hot
Meals: Lunch, dinner   Time: 30 minutes

Low Country Vegetable Fry

Many different combinations of vegetables can be used, such as cherry tomatoes, broccoli, cauliflower, carrots or sweet potatoes.

fresh mushrooms, halved

zucchini and crookneck squash, sliced
    diagonally

Vidalia onions, peeled and sliced

okra, tops cut off

spicy hot and sweet mustard

flour

yellow corn meal

salt

cayenne

oil

lemon wedges

Coat vegetables with mustard by placing them in a large bowl and tossing with adequate amount of mustard to lightly cover each piece. Dredge in mixture of equal parts flour and yellow corn meal with a small amount of salt and cayenne added. Fry in enough hot oil to cover. Drain.

Serve with lemon wedges to squeeze over vegetables and additional mustard.

Key Ingredient: Potato   Courses: Main, side
Servings: Four to six   Food Group: Vegetable
Cuisine: American   Temperature: Hot
Meals: Breakfast, lunch, dinner   Time: 45 minutes

Louie Louie Home Fries

This dish is a meal in itself. The recipe evolved when some of my special café employees asked for a brunch to surpass all others. Try combining Louie, Louie's with fresh fruit and homemade muffins.

4	large Idaho potatoes, scrubbed, diced and dried
3	tablespoons oil
1	large onion, peeled and diced
2	cloves fresh garlic, pressed
1	6-ounce jar artichoke hearts, drained and sliced
1	teaspoon basil
2	fresh tomatoes, diced
2	teaspoons spicy hot and sweet mustard
	salt and pepper to taste
½	cup grated Monterey Jack cheese
½	cup grated Parmesan cheese
1	cup sour cream

Heat oil in cast-iron or heavy skillet to medium high. Add dry potato dices and toss to coat with oil. Do not flip potatoes until a crunchy crust has formed on bottom. Cook for 10 minutes, then add onions. After cooking for 15 more minutes over medium heat, add garlic, artichoke hearts, basil, tomatoes, mustard, salt and pepper.

Preheat oven to 425°.

While still sautéing over medium heat, toss well to mix, and heat all ingredients. Cook until potatoes and onions are crisp but tender.

Remove pan from heat and sprinkle both cheeses over top. Bake in preheated oven for 10 minutes.

Place on individual serving platters and top each with a portion of sour cream.

Key Ingredient: Asparagus
Servings: Four
Cuisine: American
Meals: Brunch, lunch, dinner

Course: Main
Food Group: Vegetable, Meat
Temperature: Hot
Time: 1 hour and 15 minutes

Roulade of Spring

Surprisingly simple and inexpensive.

8   ounces fresh asparagus or broccoli spears,
       steamed until tender but crisp, and cooled

4   ounces sliced boiled or baked ham

1   teaspoon tarragon

1   tablespoon spicy hot and sweet mustard

4   eggs, beaten slightly

2   tablespoons butter

     salt and pepper to taste

1   package Pepperidge Farm frozen puff
       pastry shells

     egg wash: 1 egg slightly beaten with
       1 tablespoon water

     Basic Hollandaise Recipe (refer to Index)

Melt butter in a non-stick skillet. Add beaten eggs and scramble in butter until loosely cooked. (They will be cooked more later.) Set aside.

Slightly thaw puff pastry dough and lay on floured board or counter. Ignoring the cut lines in the pastry, roll out slightly will rolling pin to form a smooth sheet of dough. For ease in handling, keep dough chilled but pliable.

Lay slices of ham over the sheet of dough. Mix tarragon and mustard and spread evenly over ham. Spread scrambled eggs over mustard-covered ham. Lay asparagus on top of eggs close to one of the long vertical sides of dough.

Starting with the asparagus side of dough, gently roll entire package to form a roulade. Use a spatula to help if more support is necessary. Place carefully on cookie sheet, seam side down.

Preheat oven to 425°. Brush outside of egg roulade with egg wash. Place in hot oven. After 5 minutes, reduce temperature to 400° and bake for about 15 minutes more or until golden.

After removing roulade from oven, let sit for 5 minutes. Slice into rounds and top with hollandaise.

Key Ingredient: Mushrooms	Course: Side
Servings: Four to six	Food Group: Vegetable, Meat
Cuisine: Italian	Temperature: Hot
Meal: Dinner	Time: 30 minutes

Savory Stuffed Mushrooms

3 dozen large mushrooms, stems chopped and
    reserved

2 tablespoons sweet butter

2 tablespoons dry vermouth (or sherry, if Virginia
    cured ham is used)

4 very thin slices prosciutto, Westphalian ham or
    Virginia cured ham, finely chopped

6 ounces Genoa salame, finely chopped

3 scallions, finely chopped

4 tablespoons fresh parsley, finely chopped

   pinch thyme, oregano, sage, freshly ground
    black pepper

2 tablespoons spicy hot and sweet mustard

1 cup grated Fontina cheese

½ cup freshly grated Parmesan cheese (do not
    use packaged grated Parmesan)

Heat butter until very hot. Add mushrooms and cook 1 minute per side. Set aside.
Combine all other ingredients except Parmesan cheese and mix well. Stuff caps and place in a flat casserole baking dish. Bake in a 375° preheated oven for 12 minutes. Remove and sprinkle Parmesan over tops. Place under broiler for about 3 minutes or until browned. Guaranteed . . . all the mushrooms will disappear!

Key Ingredient: Potatoes
Servings: Four
Cuisine: American
Meal: Dinner

Course: Side
Food Group: Vegetable
Temperature: Hot
Time: 1 hour and 30 minutes

Soufflé Stuffed Potatoes

4   Idaho potatoes, scrubbed and baked
      45 minutes in a 375° oven

¾   cup sour cream

2   tablespoons Dijon-style mustard

2   teaspoons chives

1   teaspoon anchovy paste

1   tablespoon capers

1   egg, beaten

1   teaspoon lemon juice

½   cup freshly grated Parmesan

Cut top ⅓ off baked potatoes. Scoop out insides of bottom ⅔, leaving enough around skin to hold shape. Whip potatoes with next seven ingredients. Fill skins with stuffing and top with grated Parmesan. Bake in a 425° oven for 15 minutes.

Note: The top parts of the potatoes may be saved and used for homefries or grilled potato skins.

Key Ingredients: Eggplant, ham and cheese
Servings: Four
Cuisine: Italian influence
Meals: Brunch, lunch, dinner

Courses: First, main
Food Group: Vegetable, Meat, Dairy
Temperature: Hot
Time: 45 minutes

Aubergine (Eggplant) Sandwiches

Certainly not a traditional sandwich, this is a delicious sandwiched dish indeed!

1   medium-sized eggplant

1   teaspoon salt

8   ounces Gruyère cheese, thinly sliced

8   ounces boiled ham, thinly sliced

¼   cup spicy hot and sweet mustard

¼   cup freshly chopped parsley

2   eggs

½   cup milk

2   cups bread crumbs, preferably homemade

peanut oil for frying

Horizontally slice eggplant into ¼-inch rounds. Sprinkle with salt and let drain in colander for 20 minutes. Blot dry with paper towel.

Spread one side of each slice with mustard. Sprinkle equal portions of parsley on top of mustard. Place one slice ham and one slice cheese on top of mustard and parsley on *half* of the eggplant rounds. Top with remaining eggplant rounds, mustard side in. Press together and trim any ham or cheese that extends beyond sandwich round.

Beat egg with milk. Carefully dip each sandwich in egg mixture. Dip in bread crumbs to coat.

Heat oil over medium heat in heavy skillet. Oil level should be high enough to cover the sides of the sandwiches. When hot, gently place sandwiches in oil. Cook 5 minutes. Turn and cook 5 minutes more.

Top warm sandwiches with Rita's Rowdy Salad Dressing. (See page 108.)

Note: Sandwiches may be made up to a day ahead and kept refrigerated. Reheat in a 350° oven for 20 minutes.

Key Ingredient: Carrots Course: Side
Servings: Four Food Group: Vegetable
Cuisine: French Temperature: Hot
Meals: Brunch, lunch, dinner Time: 15 minutes

Carrot "Spaghetti" au Citron

3   carrots, peeled and shredded
1   lemon, halved lengthwise, then cut into
     paper-thin half circles
1   tablespoon spicy hot and sweet mustard
½   teaspoon dill weed
     pinch salt

Toss ingredients together and steam over boiling water 10 minutes or until al dente.

Mustard belongs to the botanical family Cruciferae, *the flowers of which have four petals arranged in the form of a cross; and to the Old World genus* Brassica, *a group which also includes cabbage, kale and collard greens. The spicy mustard plant leaves can be eaten as a salad (particularly enjoyed in spring in the southern United States) or served cooked with pot likker, the simmering liquid left from cooking leafy greens such as kale, collards or cabbage.* Cruciferae *is a huge family, containing 200 genera and more than 2,000 species . . . beloved by all botanists because it contains no poisonous members.*

Key Ingredient: Onions   Courses: Main, side
Servings: Eight   Food Group: Vegetable
Cuisine: French   Temperature: Hot
Meals: Lunch, dinner   Time: 2 hours and 30 minutes

Rita's French Onion Tart

1   9-inch pie shell (prebaked according to directions)
2   cups all-purpose flour
1   teaspoon salt
½   cup butter
3   tablespoons shortening
3 to 5   tablespoons lemon juice
1½   tablespoons spicy hot and sweet mustard

Sift together flour and salt. Cut butter and shortening into flour mixture until well blended but still coarse. Sprinkle with lemon juice. Mix and chill for 1 hour.

Roll out and place in a 9-inch pie dish. Chill 15 minutes. Line pie plate with aluminum foil and fill with uncooked beans or rice (this prevents crust from slipping). Bake at 425° for 10 minutes. Remove from oven and remove foil and beans or rice. Prick crust with fork and spread with 1½ tablespoons mustard. Return to oven and bake 10 more minutes.

Filling:
2   large onions, sliced and sautéed in 2 tablespoons sweet butter
1½   cups grated cheese (a combination of ½ Gruyère, ¼ Provolone and ¼ Monterey Jack is nice)
1   cup whipping cream
2   eggs
   dash each of cayenne, nutmeg, salt and pepper
2   tablespoons Dijon-style mustard
1   teaspoon dill weed

Make custard by mixing together whipping cream, eggs, spices, mustard and dill weed. Stir in sautéed onions. Cover baked crust with 1¼ cups grated cheese. Pour in custard. Sprinkle with remaining cheese over top. Bake in preheated 375° oven for 10 minutes. Reduce heat to 350° and bake 15 more minutes or until firm.

BREADS

Key Ingredient: Bread
Servings: Two loaves
Cuisine: American
Meals: Brunch, lunch, dinner

Courses: Bread, side
Food Group: Grain
Temperatures: Hot, warm
Time: 45 minutes

Bumpy Swirl Bread

You can allow approx. 2 hours per rising for the bread dough.

Basic French Bread (processor method):

1½	envelopes active dry yeast
2¼	cups warm (90°) water
3	cups unsifted all-purpose flour
3	cups unbleached flour
	pinch salt

In large bowl of food processor, place yeast with ¼ cup water and process 2 seconds. Add flour and process. Add salt while processing. Then add the 2 cups of water all at once. Process 16 to 20 seconds until a ball forms.

Turn dough out onto a floured surface and knead briefly. Place in a large (3 quart) greased bowl. Cover with a tea towel and place in a warm place to let rise until double in bulk.

Punch down dough to release air bubbles. Cover and let rise again until double in bulk.

Punch down again and divide and shape any way you wish. Let individual loaves rise until almost double in bulk. Slash top in several places with a razor blade. Place in a preheated 425° oven, throw two ice cubes in the bottom of the oven, and close the door. After 20 minutes, reduce heat to 375° and bake 30 to 35 minutes longer.

Directions for Bumpy Swirl Bread:

After bread dough has been punched down the second time, and rested for 10 minutes, roll out to form a rectangle.

Combine:

3	tablespoons spicy hot and sweet mustard
1	tablespoon poppy seeds
1	tablespoon sesame seeds

Spread the rolled rectangle of dough with 2 tablespoons of the mustard mixture, reserving 1 tablespoon for baking glaze. Roll up like a jelly-roll and place seam side down in a baking pan. Let rise until double in bulk.

Slash top in several places with a razor blade. Coat with a wash of 1 tablespoon mustard mixture mixed with 1 tablespoon water.

Bake according to directions for Basic French Bread.

Note: Frozen bread dough may be substituted for Basic French Bread dough.

Mustard-seed oil is the most popular cooking oil in many parts of Asia, second only to ghee. Pungent and golden when heated, mustard-seed oil is prized by Indian and Pakistani cooks. It imparts a special flavor to the chilis and spices mixed by each cook for the family curry. Even the poorest of families saves for a few ounces of the golden oil, particularly for use during the Hindu festival of Dewali, the Festival of Lights.

"The kingdom of heaven is like to a grain of mustard seed, which a man took, and sowed in his field: Which indeed is the least of all seeds; but when it is grown, it is the greatest among herbs. . . ."
—Matthew 13:31–32

Actually, the orchid seed is the smallest, but mustard seeds are indeed small. A quarter-ounce will plant a row 100 feet long; there are more than 15,000 seeds to the ounce; three quarters of a pound of black mustard seeds sown over one acre will produce 150–500 <u>million</u> second generation seeds!

120

SAUCES
GLAZES
&
MARINADES

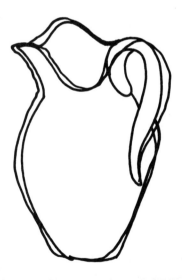

Key Ingredient: Sour cream Course: Hors d'oeuvre
Servings: Ten Temperatures: Cold, room
Meals: Brunch, snack, party Time: 5 minutes

Sauce Florentine

16 ounces sour cream
1 cup fresh spinach leaves, washed and finely chopped
2 tablespoons fresh, chopped parsley
3 scallions, finely chopped
¼ cup spicy hot and sweet mustard
1 teaspoon sesame seeds

Combine all ingredients and serve with your favorite dipping foods or on top of grilled or baked fish. Extra sauce may be stored in refrigerator.
Serving size may vary according to sauce's use.

Key Ingredient: Mayonnaise Course: Hors d'oeuvre
Servings: Eight Temperatures: Hot, cold, room
Cuisine: French Time: 5 minutes
Meals: Brunch, snack, party

Blanket du Printemps

½ cup Hellman's or homemade mayonnaise
1 teaspoon fresh lemon juice
2 tablespoons champagne or dry white wine
1 tablespoon spicy hot and sweet mustard
½ teaspoon dill weed

Mix ingredients together and use as lovely cover for fresh steamed asparagus or broccoli or as a fresh vegetable dipping sauce.
Makes ¾ cup sauce. Serving size may vary according to sauce's use.

Key Ingredient: Madeira
Servings: Four
Cuisine: American
Meals: Breakfast, brunch, dinner

Courses: Appetizer, main
Temperature: Hot
Time: 45 minutes

Mustard Sauce Madeira

A lovely sauce to top roasted or grilled meats, or eggs.

2	small onions, minced
2	tablespoons sweet butter
1½	tablespoons cornstarch dissolved in 2 tablespoons water
1	tablespoon Dijon-style mustard
⅓	cup dry red wine
⅓	cup Madeira
1¼	cup beef stock
	dash cayenne, salt and pepper

In saucepan, sauté onions in butter until browned. Add dissolved cornstarch and stir well. While stirring, add remaining ingredients. Continue stirring, bring to a boil, reduce by continuing to boil until slightly thickened. Lower heat and simmer for 20 minutes.

Basic Hollandaise Recipe

3	egg yolks, room temperature
2	tablespoons lemon juice
1	stick butter
¼	teaspoon salt
	dash cayenne

Combine yolks, lemon juice, salt and cayenne in blender. Melt butter until bubbly; don't brown. Turn blender on high speed and immediately pour butter in a slow, steady stream. Turn off blender and transfer to a bowl to keep warm.

Key Ingredient: Mustard   Time: 5 minutes
Servings: Six

Bumpy Barbecue Sauce

The spicy ingredients and fresh lime juice truly enhance the flavor of grilled chicken, beef or ribs.

¾   cup spicy hot and sweet mustard

2   tablespoons Worcestershire sauce

     juice of one fresh lime

2   teaspoons Oriental chili oil

2   teaspoons sesame seeds

Cook meat over grill until ¾ done. Mix next five ingredients together. With brush, spread over each side of meat. When finished, top with more sauce if desired. Serving size depends on size of meat.

Key Ingredient: Cranberry sauce   Temperature: Hot
Servings: Eight   Time: 10 minutes

Holiday Glaze

Glaze for pork or poultry

3   tablespoons Dijon-style mustard

2   teaspoons chives

1   large can cranberry sauce, chunky

½   cup finely chopped pecans

     grated rind of one orange

¼   cup dry red wine

Mix all ingredients together and glaze meat or poultry after it has been browned. Keep basting until meat is done. Especially good on goose or duck. Extra glaze will keep in refrigerator.

Serving size may vary according to meat size.

Key Ingredient: Orange marmalade   Temperature: Hot
Servings: Eight   Time: 5 minutes

Glaze Valencia

Great for lamb, pork or beef.

½   cup orange marmalade
⅓   cup dry red wine
⅓   cup spicy hot and sweet mustard

Spread over meat while baking, smoking or barbecuing. Serving size may vary according to meat size.

Simplicity and an abundance of flavor are characteristics I attribute to the process of marinating. A marinade is a soaking mixture consisting of an acid usually combined with an oil, plus herbs and spices to enhance flavor and give tenderness. The marinade itself, cooked or uncooked, may be used as an integral part of the sauce. For proportions, the general rule of thumb is to allow one-half cup marinade per pound of meat. The cooking process of barbecuing, grilling or smoking blends well with the flavors imparted by marinating, but roasting or broiling will also work.

Key Ingredient: Beef roast or steak   Course: Main
Servings: Eight   Food Group: Meat
Meal: Dinner   Temperature: Hot

Beef Marinade

⅔   cup dry red wine
2   tablespoons fresh lemon juice
½   cup olive oil
2   tablespoons spicy hot and sweet mustard
½   teaspoon basil
2   cloves fresh garlic, minced
2   anchovy filets, minced
1   tablespoon fresh thyme leaves (or 1 teaspoon
     dried thyme)
     salt and freshly ground pepper to taste
4   pounds beef roast or steak

Combine all ingredients to form marinade. Marinate at room temperature for at least 2 hours or overnight in refrigerator.
Cook according to recipe used.

Key Ingredient: Pork Course: Main
Servings: Eight Food Group: Meat
Meal: Dinner Temperature: Hot

Pork Marinade

juice of two fresh oranges, plus 1 tablespoon
grated orange rind
⅔ cup dry vermouth
½ cup olive oil
2 tablespoons soy sauce
2 tablespoons Dijon-style mustard
1 bay leaf
2 cloves garlic, pressed
3 to 4 pounds pork

Combine all ingredients to form marinade. Marinate at room temperature for at least 2 hours or overnight in refrigerator.
Cook according to recipe used.

Key Ingredient: Chicken Course: Main
Servings: Eight Food Group: Poultry
Meal: Dinner Temperature: Hot

Chicken Marinade

¼ cup olive oil
½ cup fresh lemon juice
1 tablespoon spicy hot and sweet mustard
2 cloves fresh garlic, pressed
¼ cup fresh snipped dill (or 2 teaspoons dried
dill weed)
¼ teaspoon salt
freshly ground pepper
3½ pounds whole or cut up chicken

Combine all ingredients to form marinade. Marinate overnight in refrigerator.
Cook or grill according to recipe used.

Key Ingredients: Beef, chicken or pork   Course: Main
Servings: Eight   Food Group: Meat
Meal: Dinner   Temperature: Hot

Marinade Cancun

Overnight marination suggested.

½   cup spicy hot and sweet mustard
6   ounces dark beer
¼   cup vinegar
1   tablespoon Worcestershire sauce
1   tablespoon chili powder
½   teaspoon cayenne
1   teaspoon salt
   beef, chicken or pork

Mix ingredients and marinate meat 4 hours or overnight in refrigerator.

Key Ingredient: Vinegar   Time: 10 minutes
Servings: Four

Basic Vinaigrette

2   tablespoons red wine vinegar
1   teaspoon lemon juice
6   tablespoons light or extra virgin olive oil
½   teaspoon salt
   freshly ground black pepper

Blend vinegar, lemon juice, salt and pepper. Vigorously whisk in a thin stream of olive oil. May be kept in a sealed jar in the refrigerator for up to 1 week.
Makes ½ cup. Serving size may vary according to use. Shake well before using.

TOKEN DESSERT

'Mustard

Key Ingredients: Chocolate, raspberries   Course: Dessert (or main, for chocoholics)
Servings: 12 to 16   Food Group: Grain
Cuisine: American   Temperature: Cold
Meal: Dessert   Time: 45 minutes

Token Chocolate Cake

Time does not include chilling and baking time. What is life without a big, fat chocolate cake? Here's one for you! The "condiments," mustard and mayonnaise, keep the cake very moist and give it a flavor similar to a German chocolate cake. The entire creation is exotic.

½   cup butter, softened

¼   cup mayonnaise

1¾   cups brown sugar

¼   cup poppy seeds

2   tablespoons spicy hot and sweet mustard

2   eggs

1   teaspoon almond extract

2   cups unsifted all-purpose flour

¾   cup cocoa

1¼   teaspoons baking soda

½   teaspoon salt

1⅓   cups water

Preheat oven to 350°. Cream butter, mayonnaise, mustard, poppy seeds and sugar until fluffy. Add eggs and almond extract, and beat until blended. Combine flour, cocoa, baking soda and salt; add them, alternating with water, to butter mixture.

Pour cake batter into greased cake pan of your choice.

For tube pan, bake for 40 to 45 minutes.

For 9-inch pans, bake 30 to 35 minutes.

Cool cake 10 minutes before removing from pan(s). Let cool completely before icing.

Filling:

¾   cup raspberry preserves, seedless if possible

¼   cup Grand Marnier liqueur

Icing:

2   cups heavy whipping cream

12   ounces semisweet chocolate

1   teaspoon vanilla extract

While cake is cooling, place cream and chocolate in saucepan and heat over medium, stirring until chocolate is melted. Pour into stainless steel or glass bowl and chill.

Mix raspberry preserves and Grand Marnier. Prick the top of each cake layer with a fork (to absorb more filling) and spread each layer with a half portion of raspberry mixture.

When cream and chocolate mixture is chilled, beat with an electric mixer until soft peaks form. Add vanilla and whip until stiff.

Spread raspberry-topped bottom layer with chocolate whipped cream. Place second layer on top. Ice the rest of the cake with chocolate whipped cream. Chill before serving.

"Mustard was not known at English tables before 1729, when an old woman, of the name of Clements, residing in Durham, began to grind the seed in a mill and to pass the flour through several processes. She kept her secret for many years to herself, during which time she sold large quantities of mustard throughout the country." From Mrs. Beaton's Book of Household Management, the heart and soul of Victorian life, published in London in 1859.

Evidently Mrs. Clements was able to keep this spicy secret only until the mid–eighteenth century, when the London-based Keen factory was known to have a flourishing mustardmaking business. This 160-year-old operation was bought out by Coleman's in 1903, and continues to be one of the largest manufacturers of mustard in the world.

About the Author

Originally from Philadelphia, Rita Calvert Cameron became interested in cooking as a child, but it wasn't until she was a young adult in California that she decided to make her career in the culinary arts. Moving rapidly from pantry person to country club co-manager, she eventually started her own restaurant in a restored art gallery.

Challenged by the California trends towards fresh ingredients and unusual food pairings, she featured her own mustards, mayonnaises and salad dressings at her Cedar Street Cafe, using their popularity as a stepping stone to developing a national marketing program.

Today, she resides in Wilmington, North Carolina with her husband, George. She markets her Calvert Cedar Street products at specialty food stores throughout the country. Her company was selected in 1985 by the Small Business Administration to represent new American products at ANUGA, the largest specialty food show in the world, held in Cologne, West Germany.

Ms. Calvert Cameron is the co-author of the "Aphrodisiac Cook Book," published in 1980.

Index

Index

Index

SPECIALTY COOKBOOKS FROM THE EAST WOODS PRESS

Quantity	Title	Each	Total
	THE AMERICAN BED & BREAKFAST COOKBOOK 200+ breakfast and brunch recipes contributed by America's finest hosts. Includes regional specialties, ethnic varieties and old family favorites.	$12.95 hardcover	
	BACKCOUNTRY COOKING, Fears "The first book to incorporate pioneer cooking methods as an alternate . . . of home and camp cooking." Sports Afield	$11.95 hardcover	
	CATCH OF THE DAY, Lentz 65,000 copies in print 150+ recipes, plus detailed species information, preparation techniques, and tricks of the trade from a renowned seafood expert.	$8.95	
	THE CATFISH COOKBOOK, Fast Recommended by Bon Appetit and Craig Claiborne, contains prize-winning recipes for an increasingly popular, high-protein fish.	$6.95	
	THE FRUCTOSE COOKBOOK, Cannon 50,000 copies sold! A perfect introduction to cooking with fructose, a natural table sugar substitute.	$5.95	
	MAKING FOOD BEAUTIFUL, Hofman Excellent recipes, garnishes and table decorating tips from a well-known food consultant. Color photos.	$9.95	
	THE PLAIN & FANCY MUSTARD COOKBOOK, Calvert 125+ delicious recipes using mustard. Everything from hors d'oeuvres to chocolate cake!	$7.95	
	SUBSTITUTING INGREDIENTS: A COOKING REFERENCE BOOK, Epstein & Klein More than 350 listings of ingredient substitutes. All kitchen tested!	$7.95	
	SWEETS WITHOUT GUILT, Cannon The perfect companion to The Fructose Cookbook, with more than 180 delectables!	$5.95	
	Subtotal		
	Shipping		
	Total Enclosed		

Prices subject to change.

Send order to:

THE EAST WOODS PRESS
429 East Boulevard • Charlotte, NC 28203

ALLOW 4 TO 6 WEEKS FOR DELIVERY

Please send my order to:

Name _____

Street _____ State _____ Zip _____

My check for $ _____ is enclosed. Or charge my MasterCard or Visa

☐ Please send me your Free book catalog.   Account No. _ _____

Expiration Date _____

For charge orders only, call our toll-free number: (800) 438-1242, ext. 102. In North Carolina (800) 532-0476. We will refund your money, excluding shipping costs, if you are dissatisfied for any reason.